Ireland, a Bicycle, and a Tin Whistle

Cycling around Ireland in search of traditional music, David Wilson follows the coastline from Presbyterian Islandmagee to Gaelic Cape Clear and back up north from Dublin to Belfast. *Ireland, a Bicycle, and a Tin Whistle* takes us on a journey across wild open spaces and through crowded pubs and festivals that pulse with energy and life. This is the Ireland of fiddles, harps, and flutes, butterflies on bog roads, Country-and-Irish songs, Ulster Fries, storytelling, yarnspinning, and jigs and reels till the crack of dawn.

As he travels through the North, Wilson gets beneath the surface to portray both the tragedy and comedy of everyday life inside the Protestant and Catholic communities. Aware of the polarized image that each side has of the other, he emphasizes the importance of finding common ground and asserting the middle against the extremes.

Just as traditional Irish music is characterized by ornamentations and elaborations on a melodic theme, *Ireland, a Bicycle, and a Tin Whistle* is full of variations and wanderings on the theme of the trip itself. And just as traditional Irish musicians will follow a sad slow air with a lively foot-tapping reel, Wilson's mood ranges from the nostalgic and reflective to the irreverent and mischievous. If there is a lament in one ear, there is always a song in the other.

DAVID A. WILSON is a professor in the Celtic Studies Program and the Department of History at the University of Toronto. He has written five books and is currently working on a biography of Darcy McGee.

JUSTIN PALMER is a freelance illustrator and puppeteer.

Ireland
a Bicycle
and a Tin Whistle

DAVID A. WILSON

ILLUSTRATED BY JUSTIN PALMER

McGill-Queen's University Press
Montreal & Kingston • London • Ithaca

© McGill-Queen's University Press 1995
ISBN 0-7735-1343-4 (cloth)
ISBN 0-7735-1344-2 (paper)

Legal deposit fourth quarter 1995
Bibliothèque nationale du Québec

Printed in Canada on acid-free paper

Reprinted in paperback 1996, 1998, 2001

Published simultaneously in the European Union by Blackstaff Press
ISBN 0-85640-565-5

McGill-Queen's University Press acknowledges the financial support of
the Government of Canada through the Book Publishing Industry Development
Program (BPIDP) for its activities. It also acknowledges the support of the Canada
Council for the Arts for its publishing program.

Canadian Cataloguing in Publication Data

Wilson, David A., 1950–
Ireland, a bicycle, and a tin whistle
ISBN 0-7735-1343-4 (bound) –
ISBN 0-7735-1344-2 (pbk.)

1. Ireland – Description and travel.
2. Wilson, David A., 1950–   – Journeys – Ireland.
I. Title.

DA978.2.W55 1995   914.1504'824   C95-900543-9

Typeset in Minion 10.5/13 by Caractéra inc., Quebec City

"Whiskey on a Sunday" (The Puppet Song – Seth Davey), words and music by Glyn
Hughes, used by permission of TRO Essex Music Ltd.

"The Rambling Rover," words and music by Andy M. Stewart, used by permission of

For Zsuzsa

Contents

PORTSTEWART
RATHLIN ISLAND
BALLYCASTLE
CUSHENDALL
CARNLOUGH BAY
ISLANDMAGEE
WHITEHEAD

THE
SKERRY
INN

BELFAST

GLENCOLUMBKILLE

SLIGO

WESTPORT
COUNTY MAYO

CLIFDEN
THE PUNCTURE
GALWAY

DUBLIN

INISHEER
COUNTY CLARE
MILTOWN MALBAY
MULLAGH

LISTOWEL
(ALCOHOLIC FOG)

DINGLE
COUNTY KERRY
CORK

BALTIMORE
CAPE CLEAR

IRELAND

NORTH

The poet must feel and understand that rapid fluctuation of spirits, that unaccountable mixture of gloom and levity, which composes the character of my countrymen.

THOMAS MOORE

I have found life a rewarding, exciting, enchanting and sometimes a terrifying experience, and I've enjoyed it completely. A lament in one ear, maybe; but always a song in the other. And to me, life is simply an invitation to live.

SEAN O'CASEY

I'll play you a sad old air if you like, as long as you don't mind a good fast reel coming up after.

FIDDLE PLAYER, LISTOWEL, COUNTY KERRY

Whitehead

"We're all fuckin' mental around here," said the man across the table, with fierce civic pride. I am sitting in the Whitecliff Inn, Whitehead, County Antrim, my starting point, and holding steady at the speed of six pints an hour with the Lost Souls, the local chapter of the Northern Irish branch of the Hell's Angels. Earlier in the evening, they'd picked up a bottle of wine apiece at the off-licence, taken me with them to the seafront, downed each bottle in one, and flung the empties into the sea. Now, at the Whitecliff, they were getting down to some serious drinking; it was like a Commando Course in Applied Alcohol Consumption.

In between making plans for their annual midnight motorbike run over the Carrick-a-Rede rope bridge, the Lost Souls were telling me about their world in Whitehead. They knew that I'd been born here,

that our family had moved away to England when I was still in primary school, and that at some indeterminate date we'd gone on to Canada. "The Returned Yank," they'd rechristened me, not being given to trouble themselves with pedantic North American distinctions of nationality. Besides, they all had nicknames of their own; there was Ripcord and Fingers and Deadman and Houdini, who became Hou-fuckin'-dini as the evening progressed. They were only trying to make me feel at home.

And in some ways, going back to Whitehead was like going home. Leaving the world of the Whitecliff, I could walk along paths where I had walked as a child – down from 83 Islandmagee Road to the school by the sea, bundled up against the cold, ears raw with the shrill cry of the wind through telephone wires on darkening winter days. And from here to the Marine Parade and the promenade that leads to the Blackhead Lighthouse, where you could slide your hands along the railings, put messages in old wine bottles that drifted in from the sea, and sail wooden boats that danced on the waves before being swallowed up into the darkness and the drownings.

Along the seafront now, with the thick smell of seaweed in the air, beneath the cliffs and towards the caves. At high tide, the sea surged and crashed inside them, breaking against the rocks and echoing like thunder. If you waited long enough, until the rush had receded, you could make your way down, heart beating faster over slippery blackness, and stand where the sea had swirled. And if you looked upwards, you could just make out the crevice where a wandering teacher of old, driven mad by other people's laughter, had taken shelter from the world, and shivered to death in the dampness that came seeping out of the walls.

Beyond the caves, the path curved around Blackhead Point and twisted its way up steep steps to the lighthouse. As you climbed them, you could see the chimney-stack rock in the next bay and the farms of Islandmagee that sloped down to the sea. At the top, on a good day, you could see the glints of sun-reflected light on the Rinns of Galloway, and the hills of County Down on the far side of Belfast Lough. On the lighthouse wall, beside a corrugated-iron cottage, was the rusted remnant of a sign: DANGER. FOGHORN MAY

4

SOUND WITHOUT WARNING. "What'll happen if we're here when the horn goes off?" I had asked my dad when the sign was new. "We'll go deaf," he replied, cheerily; the rest of the day had been spent in silent terror. But I went back by myself, praying that the horn would not go off; it never did. I went back to watch the fishing boats, and to see the ships going out from Belfast harbour.

And one day, I was on one of those ships. There were cranes and cars and lorries and concrete docks; there were crowded gangways and waving arms; there were men in white jackets cracking jokes and showing us to our cabin. "The sea looks very rough," whispered my mother to my father; she did not want to leave. "Sure it's as calm as a millpond," he replied; the future would be better in England. I wondered what a millpond was, and played with the water taps in the cabin sink, off and on, off and on, off and on, wanting to stay, wanting to leave.

In some ways, it was like going home; in others, it was like stepping onto a different planet. "Nobody cares about religion here," Fingers was telling me; but he could name the religion of everyone at the table. Outside, staring across the sea to Scotland, was the Glasgow Rangers Supporters Club – traditionally, a Protestant team for a Protestant people. The boulders on the beach had been spray-painted with the initials UVF, the Ulster Volunteer Force, the people who'd fight Britain to remain British. The broken-down benches along the promenade had been knifed with the letters FTP, Fuck the Pope. There was a faint smell of urine in the air.

The Catholics were in the minority; they had to be careful. They might be seen as decent neighbours, or they might be seen as embodiments of the abstract republican menace; on occasions, they could be seen as both at once. I'd witnessed the transformation myself, a few days before, at the Magheramorne Social Club down the road. We were all dancing and laughing with each other, until the evening finished with the customary rendition of the National Anthem. "God Save Our Gracious Queen, Long Live Our Noble Queen, God Save Our Queen," went the singer. As the band crescendoed into the next line, a forest of fists was raised to the cry of "For God and Ulster," and a Catholic man who'd been close-dancing with a Protestant woman suddenly found her fist in front of his face; he had momentarily become the Enemy. And when it was over, everyone carried on talking as if nothing had happened, as if we were all on the surface. It was safer that way.

We were talking about it in the Whitecliff. "When there's mixed company," said one of the Catholics at the bar, "it's wrong to play the Queen; they should forget about anthems and just go home." His Protestant friends were not amused; to them, it was a statement of disloyalty. Voices became louder, tempers shorter. After he left, someone was waiting for him; the next day, he could hardly raise his arm for the bruises. "He should have known better than to have said that," a Protestant friend told me when he heard the news. "I mean, it's our National Anthem, and people living here should respect it. And if they don't respect it, they can go and live somewhere else. I mean, if I was living in the South, I would respect their anthem. So I would expect people living here to respect ours." And so it goes – "ours" and "theirs" – in the patterns of the past and the faces of the future.

Distant, half-forgotten memories are stirred – the school playground, black shoes running on asphalt, and the new boy from the South. "Popehead, Popehead," the kids would chant and taunt; sometimes, a mob of uniforms would surround and smother him, pushing him over and jeering, pushing him over and cheering. "I'm not a Catholic," he would cry in desperation. And he wasn't; there were none of them in our schools, and there were none of us in theirs. But he was from the South, and the South was full of Popeheads, and Popeheads were bad, and that was enough.

I remember the breadman who came by every fortnight in a battered old white van, selling loaves to the mothers and giving out last week's leftover rolls to the kids who crowded around him. "Who wants a sticky bun?" he would ask. "Me! I do! Give us one, mister!" And he would laugh and say "All right, c'mon then, say after me: 'Long Live King Billy! To Hell with the Pope!'" And we all did, Protestants and Catholics alike, as he handed out stale, sugar-coated rewards for our loyalty and our apostasy. "I wish I had a penny – what for? what for?" he would sing. "To buy a rope and hang the Pope and fight for Garibaldi." Garibaldi? I hadn't a clue. But then, I hadn't a clue about the Pope, either.

6

As far as my parents were concerned, this was all so much nonsense. My father came from a Protestant family, but had made the break during the war; he served side by side with Catholics in the Fleet Air Arm and came to realize that when push came to shove, they were all in it together. Besides, the priests handed out extra cigarettes to all the Catholics in the squadron; from the moment he found that out, he lied through his teeth and pretended to be Catholic himself. After that, he never saw things in quite the same way again.

"I'll tell you this," I overheard my mother saying, "I would not like to be a Catholic in Northern Ireland." She was different, too; she was English. The local Orange Lodge marched past our house on the Twelfth of July, black suits and bowler hats, sashes and banners, flutes and fifes, boys who twirled the stick and men who pounded the drums, sending out their messages: this is our territory and Ulster is British and you'd bloody well better not forget it. She was horrified; for her, being British meant being decent, not waving your fist in someone else's face. "What are they doing?" I asked. "They're just a lot of silly men," she said; "don't take any notice of them."

But when you're born and brought up here, you can't help but take notice of them; they make themselves impossible to ignore. It becomes difficult to imagine a world without Protestants and Catholics, Unionists and Nationalists, us and them. I'd left when I was a kid, and my parents were vaguely liberal; I found it impossible to identify with either side. And yet, the more time I spent in Northern Ireland, the more I felt the pressure to conform, to move out of my No-Man's Land and come down clearly on one side or the other.

People would start probing to find out which foot I kicked with; there were indirect questions about where I went to school, or where in Belfast my father was from, or where he'd worked before moving to England. On the rare occasions when the subject of religion actually came out into the open, I would admit to being an agnostic; this, however, was dismissed as little more than a cowardly form of evasion. "Yes, yes," you could almost hear them mutter, "but are you a Protestant agnostic or a Catholic agnostic?" What can you say? That you keep an open mind about the existence of God, but if there is one, then he (or she) is a Protestant? In any case, being an agnostic puts you in the worst of all possible worlds: for the diehard Protestants, it's even worse than being a Catholic; and for the diehard Catholics, it's even worse than being a Protestant. Agnosticism ranks far above atheism in the Scale of Disapproval, since atheists at least have the courage of their convictions to stand up for what they don't believe in.

People started defining me in ways that I would never have defined myself. I was not Catholic; therefore, I must be Protestant. Shortly after I returned to Whitehead, I was having tea with a Catholic family – old friends of my parents – in front of the television. There were pictures of the Royal Black Preceptory, the most Orange of all Orangemen, marching through nearby Larne. I made some casual comment on the "silly men" theme, and they decided to take me up on it. "Still, they're your boys all the same when it comes to the crunch," said the husband, teasingly. "At the end of the day, you'll all be on the same side of the barricades." I didn't know what to say; I couldn't imagine myself on either side of the barricades. "You've got to be kidding," I replied; "there's no way I'd ever fight with that lot." "So, you're one of us now, are you?" asked the wife, with the faintest implication of reproach, that I was betraying my "own" people. "No," I said, "I wouldn't be fighting with you, either." There was a long pause, followed by the verdict: "So," she pronounced, "you're confused."

You're one of us, you're one of them, or you're confused. But I'd been living long years in Canada, where confusion about Ireland grew with each wave of the Atlantic and each year of distance. During the nineteenth century, the Irish had been the largest ethnic group in English-speaking British North America; Toronto was known as the Belfast of Canada. Old-world rivalries had travelled to the New; there had been sporadic Orange and Green riots right up to the 1870s. Gradually, though, the colours faded; both groups began to sink their differences, and merged into a common Canadianism. Each side's image of the other became blurred; sharp assertions of supremacy evolved into hazy folk traditions.

If you wanted confusion, you could find it in Canada all right. A few months after our family immigrated, we stumbled across an

Orange Parade in the Ottawa Valley outback – a parade with a difference. King Billy was mounted on a time-worn brown horse, instead of the time-honoured white; the banners were tattered and the songs had changed. In your orthodox Orange Parade, you would hear the old standards like "The Protestant Boys" and "The Sash My Father Wore." They were played so often that you could imagine them on one of those mail-order television commercials: Marching Orangemen on the right, song-titles on the left, and the ingratiating voice over the medley of tunes – "Thrill to Civil and Religious Liberty on the 'Green Grassy Slopes of the Boyne' … Defeat the Dark Forces of Rome, Superstition and the Antichrist with 'Croppies Lie Down.'" But there were none of these songs here. Mainstream music had taken over the sound system; the Irish Rovers carried the day. "Oh, it is the biggest mix-up that you have ever seen," they sang; "My father he was Orange and my mother she was Green." And they followed it up with "The Unicorn," the Irish Rovers' greatest hit, with its "green alligators and long-necked geese" – a song actually written by Shel Silverstein, a Jewish story-teller from New York, probably to wreak some kind of private revenge on the Irish in North America.

After the marching and the music, an Orange Parade would normally be addressed by the Grand Master of the District Lodge, who would talk at considerable length about God, Ulster, and the British Empire. Not in the Ottawa Valley; here, they did things differently. The oration was delivered by none other than the local Catholic priest – something that the folks back in Belfast might have found a shade suspect. And if his presence was unexpected, his message was unusual. "Let us give the lie to those people who say that Protestants and Catholics cannot get on with each other," he said. "The very fact that we have come together today is living proof that we can and will coexist peacefully." Why, then, was there so much conflict in Northern Ireland? The answer was clear for those who had eyes to see: "What we are witnessing in Ireland today is an insidious and sinister Marxist plot, aimed at nothing less than the destruction of civilization as we know it."

There were strange mutations in this strange new world: the identifiable enemy had become communist rather than Catholic;

9

the conspiracy against civil and religious liberty had become centred in Moscow rather than Rome; the Presbytery and the Pope must stand together against the Godless hordes. Meanwhile, in the background, the Irish Rovers played on.

Back in Whitehead, there was a different kind of ecumenicalism – the ecumenicalism of alcohol. The Lost Souls at the Whitecliff never slackened their pace; apart from anything else, the custom of buying rounds meant that there was no room to escape. And this is where another difference between the New World and the Old enters the picture. If you go into a pub in Canada, you will sit with your friends, order your own drinks from the waiter or waitress, and pay individually. Not so in Ireland, and definitely not so in Whitehead. Hou-fuckin'-dini would step up to the bar, order a dozen pints, and distribute them to the group; ten minutes later Ripcord would follow suit, and so it would go all around the circle until we were back at the beginning, ready to repeat the procedure. It was a lethal mixture of communal pressure and individual competition; only those with leather livers would make it past the age of thirty.

It didn't matter whether you could keep up or not; the pints piled up in front of you anyway. After a while, I began to fall off the pace and resorted to desperate face-saving measures. I remembered a jingle that my father had taught me just before I reached drinking age: "Beer on whiskey, very risky; Whiskey on beer, never fear." Never fear; I switched immediately to shots of Bushmills. In retrospect, this was a mistake. At first, the whiskey slid down my throat, smooth as syrup; never underestimate your father's wisdom, I thought. But slowly the world as I knew it began to twist and turn into different dimensions; my mind was revolving with the room, the Lost Souls were spinning around me faster and faster, and my body was beginning to sink under the growing force of gravity. Somewhere in the distance, as if through an echo chamber, a voice was shouting: "That's it, lads, closing time, finish it up! Have yous no homes to go to? C'mon, on your bikes!" Ripcord and Deadman went to the bar to buy some carry-outs, cans of lager for home consumption; for them, the evening was only just beginning. I'd have to be carried out as well; I was slumped in the corner like a sack of potatoes. "He's a beaten docket," someone said, hoisting me into his arms and hauling me to his home.

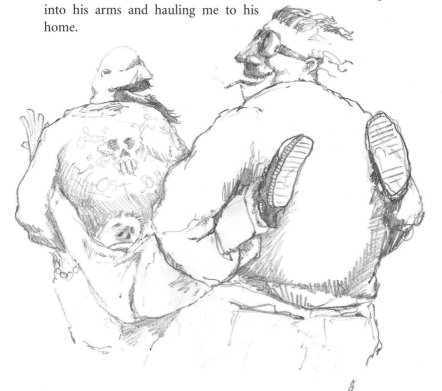

After several days of blackness, I re-emerged into the light, blinking heavily against the sun and steadying myself against the railings – another casualty of the devil-may-care, drink-your-faces-off-and-die world of the Lost Souls. A motorbike pulled up and Ripcord dismounted. "You're playin' tonight in Hooks's Bar," he told me. "Be there at eight." The word had got out that I played the guitar, and the boys had booked me to provide the Saturday night's entertainment in Ballycarry. Hooks's Bar was a shack of a place, with two rooms – a sparse, barren bar-room that stank of disinfectant, and a lounge bar that looked much the same except for a thick, stained, red carpet. I'd be playing in the lounge, I was told, but I could have a few drinks in the bar before I got going. Here, I got chatting to Billy, a large, avuncular man who'd recently retired from the cement works down the road. Billy was blunter than most people you'd meet. "It doesn't matter a damn to me what religion you are," he said; "I don't care what any man's religion is." The meaning was clear: it mattered; he cared. "But just out of interest, like, what would you call yourself?"

Now, this was hard-core Protestant territory, with red, white, and blue kerbstones and Ulster flags, an overspill area from Belfast's Loyalist Shankill Road; only someone with pronounced suicidal tendencies would have admitted to being anything other than a Protestant. I do not have such tendencies. "I'd call myself a Protestant," I said, temporarily abandoning my agnosticism in the interests of a long and healthy life. "Of course you're a fuckin' Protestant," said Billy. "What I want to know is, are you Church of Ireland or Presbyterian?" I guessed that I was Church of Ireland, and fortunately I guessed right; there were smiles and handshakes and drinks all round. If religious differences didn't exist, it wouldn't take these boyos long to invent them.

Time to start the evening's show. I ventured into the lounge, carrying a borrowed guitar. There were only three people in the place, a table of women with their beehives and babychams, clustered in conversation, all powder and perfume and make-up. I nodded hello; they nodded back, glanced at each other, shook their heads, and left. To while away the time, I began to play a few classical pieces on the guitar; the music of Bach and Tarrega wafted over the thick, red carpet and the empty chairs. Every so often, the lounge door would open, a face would peer in the room, and instantly disappear.

Then they came in – three lads, hard as nails, arms tattooed with UVF, GOD AND ULSTER, and MOTHER, fingers with LOVE and HATE, faces scarred with Saturday night fights. As they sat down with their half-uns and their wee nips, one of them turned to me and said in a slow, staccato monotone: "Play us something we can all sing along to." It was one of the most menacing requests I had ever heard.

It was also one of the most challenging. Most of the songs I knew fell into the tortured, introspective, "nobody-understands-me-and-I-haven't-been-laid-in-months" genre that was so popular back in the sixties. Stay calm, don't panic, think clearly; besides, if the worst comes to the worst, Billy's in the other room, right, and Billy and I are both Church of Ireland, right? "All right lads, no problem. How about 'The Streets of London'?" "Whatever you like, Davy boy, your pleasure," came the response, with enough sinister undertones to cause a collective movement of bowels. No choice; into the song I went, trying to look as harmless and inoffensive as possible. And for a few brief moments, I thought I was going to get away with it. "That was fuckin' brilliant," said one; something of an overreaction, I thought, but it would not have been politic to have complained.

But the sweet and innocent look had jogged dangerous and potentially disastrous musical memories. "Do you know any John Denver songs?" went the Slow Voice from Hell. Not a single one; totally fucked; game over; babbling with fear. "Sorry lads, I know of his songs, but I never actually got round to learning any myself, although I always meant to, and I think they're very good, but they're out of my voice range, and I always thought I'd murder them." Not acceptable. "You *must* know John Denver, Davy," came the reply. "*Everybody* knows John Denver." "'Country Roads,'" said his friend; "play 'Country Roads.' Or you'll wake up fuckin' dead in the morning." It came as something of a surprise to learn that John Denver had such devoted and loyal admirers; nor had I suspected that the Ballycarry division of his fan club would tear me limb from limb for the crime of pretending to be a folksinger while being unable or unwilling to sing "Country Roads" – as clear a case of fraud as you could find.

Try to change the subject. "Look lads, I play instrumentals mainly; let me do one of those for you instead." Momentary respite. "Aye, all right; show us what you can do." I started playing a frenetic version of "Classical Gas," and followed it up immediately with a folk-blues classic from the sixties called "Angie" – a tune that all would-be guitarists from that era practised repeatedly in their bedrooms to gain admission to the Inner Circle of Talented Guitarists. ("He's good on the guitar, but how fast can he play 'Angie'?") By the time I'd worked it out, it was too late; everyone else had moved on to "Stairway to Heaven." But, having taken the time and trouble to learn it, I wasn't going to jettison it from my already limited repertoire – and it seemed that it just might save me now. "That was dead on, fuckin' brill, so it was," they said; it looked like I was going to make it through the night after all. "Well, if you liked that one," I asked, "would you like to hear a few more like it?" "Whatever you like, Davy boy, your pleasure." I moved quickly into a finger-style instrumental version of "God Bless the Child," which I'd cribbed from a record a few months earlier; it was technically difficult, but had a gentle jazz-blues feel guaranteed to soothe the soul of a psycho-killer – or so I thought. Half way through the second verse, one of them stood up. He did not look soothed. He walked over and curled his fingers – H-A-T-E – over the fretboard, deadening the strings. He leant over me, looked me in the eye, and said very softly and very slowly: "You've shown us that you can play the fuckin' guitar, Davy. Now play a John Denver song."

And I did. From the dark recesses of my past, from too many nights in northern Ontario bars listening to the Worst Country and Western Songs in the World, from sheer unadulterated terror, the chords and the words started to come out – and even to come out in roughly the right order – "West Virginia, mountain mamma, take me home, country roads." Take me home ... take me home. They did not say it was fuckin' brill; in fact, they looked rather upset. "I'm desperate for a pint," I said, seeking a socially acceptable escape route. "I'll be back in a few minutes."

Across the hall and into the bar-room, things were hopping and beer was spilling; there would be more disinfectant on the floor before the night was over. "What about ye?" said Billy, calling me over; I stuck with him for protection for the rest of the night. "See 'American Pie,'" someone said. "See Sammy over there. He plays it." The guitar was brought in from the lounge and handed to a man with slicked-back hair, a man from the brylcreem generation when coifs were coifs and rockers put rubber hosepipe inside leather pants. Sammy smiled like Elvis, and moved smoothly into an American-accented version of the song, which everyone knew off by heart, and sang at full throttle.

Then somebody asked me for Ralph McTell's "From Clare to Here," a nostalgic song about an Irish labourer in London wishing he was back in County Clare. It begins with four lads sharing a room and working hard for the "crack." Not to be confused with illegal mind-blowing substances, the "crack" in Ireland means legal, mind-blowing conversation, full of laughter, diversion, and devilment. "The crack was ninety," people will say when they're describing the peak of the evening; it doesn't get any higher than that. "Why not?" you might ask. "You can't get higher than ninety," you'll be told, as if only a complete fool would ask such a stupid question. Anyway, the lads in the song are working hard for the crack, and all seems safe enough. But the next line takes you into dangerous territory, here in Hooks's Bar: "Sleeping late on Sundays,

I never get to Mass." "If you sing that song," a friend had warned me before the evening began, "whatever you do, change those words; say 'wishing it would last' or something like that, but don't on any account mention the M word." After what had happened in the lounge, I was taking no chances.

It was just as well. A few minutes later, someone started to sing "Willie McBride," a beautiful, haunting Eric Bogle song about the waste of lives in World War One. No one was paying much attention until the singer came to the part about a nineteen-year-old who had "joined the great fallen in 1916." Suddenly, all hell broke loose. "We're not having any fuckin' rebel Papist republican songs in here, that's for bloody sure," came a Neanderthal cry; the guitar was in danger of being splintered over a head. 1916. The Easter Rising. The blood sacrifice on behalf of Catholic Nationalism. Not something that would go down well in a Protestant bar. "Leave him alone, for fuck's sake," someone else shouted. "It's got nothing to do with the Easter Rising. It's about the Somme, you fuckin' moron." 1916. The Battle of the Somme. The blood sacrifice on behalf of Protestant Unionism. That was a different kettle of bloody fish altogether. Things began to settle; the singer was allowed to continue and received a generous round of applause at the end.

Another close escape on a Ballycarry Saturday night.

At the end of the evening, though, something remarkable happened. They didn't finish with the Queen; may-

be they were so entrenched in their Loyalism that they didn't need to prove it to themselves. Instead, they wound up with a rousing rendition of "Jerusalem," the hymnal version of the William Blake poem:

> And did those feet in ancient times
> Walk upon England's pastures green?
> And was the holy lamb of God
> On England's pleasant pastures seen?
> I will not cease from mental fight
> Nor shall my sword sleep in my hand
> Till we have built Jerusalem
> In England's green and pleasant land.

Everyone joined in – Billy, the lads from the lounge, Sammy/Elvis, the Neanderthaler, the singer who'd nearly become the latest martyr of 1916 – and they filled the room with raw emotion; it was a truly moving moment. But what kind of Jerusalem were they building here, on an east Antrim hillside, surrounded by Papists, sheltered by the Somme, singing John Denver?

Sweet Carnlough Bay

And so, with the strains of "Jerusalem" still running through my mind, I left Whitehead and cycled along the country roads of green and pleasant Islandmagee, en route to Cushendall. Islandmagee is not actually an island; it is a peninsula that hooks upwards from Belfast Lough towards Larne. The Middle Road takes you through rolling hills, past well-kept farms with brambled hedges and stone gateposts that look like miniature fortresses. If you turn off to the east, you can make your way to the path that runs beneath Gobbins Head, winding through tunnelled-out rock and stumbling over broken stones, ledged between sheer cliffs and the sea. Many years ago, with the coming of the railway, the walk attracted tourists from all over the country, even from London; there was a tubular bridge to carry you across one rift in the rocks, and a strung-together suspension bridge to take you over another. Now, hardly anyone comes here; there are no signposts, the path is crumbling into the sea, and the bridges have rusted and rotted away.

Most travellers bypass Islandmagee. The road doesn't lead anywhere except back again, and there is no car ferry to take you over the water to Larne. But it is perfect cycling country; there is little traffic, apart from the occasional Lost Soul, and the hills aren't too steep – although the drops down to Portmuck harbour and the beach at Brown's Bay will burn the rubber on your brakes and change the pressure in your ears. This is a place with a strong sense of community and cohesion. "Kick an Islandmagee man," the saying goes, "and the whole island limps." And, beneath the neat and tidy Presbyterian exterior, it is full of the unexpected; there are prehistoric, Gaelic, and Lowland Scottish roots here, twisting together in strange and surprising ways.

The most visible sign of the prehistoric past appears at the head of the peninsula, in the form of an ancient burial site known as the Druid's Altar. The stones stand incongruously in the front garden of a modern cottage, leaning together like lawn ornaments from another world. Some of the first people who settled in Ireland came into the northeast; among those who passed this way, at least a few remained huddled on these hills, gazing across the sea to the land they had left behind. A few miles to the south, there is a faint trace of another tradition that has virtually vanished from the area. As you cycle out of Whitehead, you pass a shop called the Rinka. The shop used to be a dance-hall; the Irish word for dancing is *rince*; the phonetic pronunciation in English is rinka. But apart from the occasional placename, there is nothing left in Islandmagee of the old Gaelic order that was swamped by the Ulster Scots some four centuries ago.

Elsewhere in Northern Ireland, the overlay of Protestant culture on Gaelic foundations has produced some ironic consequences. A friend of mine told me about a staunch Loyalist who was infuriated by the law that enabled Catholics to rename their streets in the Gaelic language. "Let them try that around where I live," he said, "and just see what bloody well happens." "Why, where do you live?" asked my friend. "Ballyhackamore," came the indignant reply.

There are no Catholics in Islandmagee, and there have not been since the middle of the seventeenth century. Back in 1641, there was a Catholic rising in the north of Ireland against the settlers; in Protestant culture, folk memories of the massacres and atrocities persist into the present. Then, as now, there were reprisals – including the slaughter of fifty Catholics who were living on the peninsula. In the Islandmagee imagination, the story expanded to the point where hundreds of Catholics were driven to their death over the cliffs at Gobbins Head. To this day, it is said that the nettles in the fields above the Gobbins have dark red leaves from the blood of the Catholics who were slain.

It is the myth of a community that responded to crisis by destroy-ing the perceived enemy in its midst; the pattern is depressingly familiar. Today, in Northern Ireland, the vast majority of Protestants and Catholics live in their own communities, insulated and isolated from the other. Catholics living in Protestant housing estates have been burnt out of their homes; Protestants living in Catholic territory near the border have been forced out of their farms. Each community defines itself against the other; the land is strewn with blood-red nettles.

And yet, in their very separateness, Protestants and Catholics are much more alike than they realize; in many ways, they are divided by what they have in common. Both sides see themselves as threatened minorities – the Protestants as a minority in the island of Ireland, the Catholics as a minority in the state of Northern Ireland. Both sides take their religion straight up, and don't want their children exposed to the "wrong" faith; the level of support for segregated education runs high across the Protestant-Catholic divide. Both sides tend to view politics as a zero-sum game, in which a victory for one side automatically means a defeat for the other, and compromise is only victory or defeat in disguise. The key words are "either" and "or," not "both" and "together." Even the symbols are similar. If Protestant kerbstones are painted in the red, white, and blue of the Union Jack, their Catholic counterparts are painted the green, white, and orange of the Irish Tricolour. And if Protestant graffiti proclaim FTP, the Catholics reply with FTQ. It's like living in a world of mirror images, where each side sees the image, but neither sees the mirror.

Here, in Islandmagee, there are few face-to-face encounters with real or imagined enemies. Looking out across the Irish Sea, away from the beaten track, overwhelmingly Protestant, the peninsula could easily be mistaken for a fragment of Scotland rather than a part of Ireland. Back in the seventeenth century, when King James I prevented the Irish Presbyterians from practising their religion, hundreds of them rowed back and forth across the sea to Scotland every Sunday for communion. The Scottish connection remains powerful; you can hear it in the rhythms of speech, and you can feel it in the folk traditions that permeate the place. As they crossed the sea, the people who settled in Islandmagee carried witches, fairies, spirits, and ghosts with them. "In no part of Ireland," ran a government report from the 1830s, "are the people more generally and inveterately superstitious than here."

There were stories of hauntings, fairy music, fortune-telling, magic, and counter-magic. To prevent your cows from becoming bewitched, you had to hang a "witch stone" above their heads in the byre. To protect yourself from evil spells, you had to strew your farmyard with marigolds on May Day. To cure diseases, you could call on the local "wise woman," whose charms and incantations would result in supernatural healing. Even today, it is said, the "wee folk" are about at night. They leave fairy rings, circles of dark grass around thorn bushes; if you step inside, you will be cursed. But you will receive good luck if you cross a baby's hand with silver, or if the first person entering your house on New Year's Day has dark hair.

Before they moved to Whitehead, my parents spent several years in Islandmagee, living in a farm labourer's cottage without electricity or running water. Although they were outsiders from the modern, industrial, urban world, it wasn't long before they began to succumb to the supernatural. "If ever you see a cow with two heads," my father was told, "you have come face to face with the Devil himself." He thought no more about it, until one night, walking home alone, he saw a still figure in the distance, silhouetted against the darkening sky – the shape of a cow, with a head where its head should have been, and a head where its tail should have been. "What did you do?" I asked. "I ran like hell," he said. "And I didn't stop running until I was back home with the door locked behind me, and the key safe in my pocket."

Every day, the bus would come from Belfast, wending its way through narrow roads, stopping at the different farmhouses. And every day, groups of Islanders would gather at Ballydown Hill to follow its progress, to see who was coming and who was going. At first, my mother found this to be rather eccentric; living in London, she'd seen a good few buses in her time. But after a few weeks, she found herself looking forward to the event; it became one of the highlights of the day, waiting for the bus and chatting with the neighbours, and having tea and biscuits together in someone's house. When my parents bought a paraffin stove – the first one in Islandmagee, no less – they found that they were suddenly at the centre of the social scene. More and more people dropped by, ostensibly to give their regards, but actually to inspect the latest example of modern technology, to find out how well it worked and how much it cost. Between the bus and the stove, the gossip and the curiosity, rhythms were established and friendships were formed; little by little, they were being drawn into the community.

Among their friends was John Napier, a farm labourer from just down the road. "Sure your mother was just a wee bairn when she had you," he said when I called round to see him. He pulled out faded photographs, put the kettle on, fed me a plate of sandwiches, and took me on a tour of the district. The cottage had been bulldozed away; the paraffin stove had long since given up the ghost. John decided to show me off to the neighbours and took me on a house-to-house visit. At each place, the same ritual was enacted. "D'ye recognize this fellow?" he would ask as he brought me in. The neighbours would shake their heads in embarrassment; the last time they'd seen me I was only six months old, and I'd changed a bit in the meantime. He let them dangle on the hook for a while. "You've met him before, you know," he would say; meanwhile, I was just standing there, trying not to look too stupid. Then, he would reveal his Secret Knowledge: "D'ye remember the Wilsons who lived over by Miss Ross? Well, this is their wee boy." Handshakes and smiles all round; invitations for tea. "You're raising a nice smell," John would say when the scones came out of the oven; the hosts would nod back approvingly and bring out still more. Every plate had to be finished; there was no choice in the matter. Scones, scones, and more scones: it was the Presbyterian version of the Lost Souls' drinking syndrome, an easy switch from alcoholism to foodaholism.

Still, being on a bicycle gives you a chance of working off the calories and maintaining some kind of equilibrium between the pints consumed and the miles travelled. After parting company with John Napier and his neighbours, I freewheeled down the hill, past the Druid's Altar, to take the boat to Larne. While I was waiting, one of the Islanders told me a bit about the place. Many centuries ago, he said, St Patrick himself had passed this way, blessed the ferry, and assured his fellow travellers that no one would ever drown in the crossing. But the blessing somehow wore off during the last century; in a sudden storm, the boat capsized and all the passengers went over. Three of them managed to hold on and were rescued by a young lad who had seen the accident from the shore, and who went out to get them in his father's fishing boat. But the fourth was swept under by the tide and never came up; they found his body by Ballylumford shore, just down the road. He was sixteen years old.

Eventually, the ferry arrived – a glorified rowing boat with an outboard motor, coming across Larne Lough. "Have a good crossing, now," he said cheerfully as he strolled back to his house. I checked the sky carefully for approaching squalls, took the measure of the wind, and lowered my bicycle onto the boat. Before I knew it, I was on the other side; St Patrick was back on form. The captain moored the boat for a year and a day, although he would be returning in an hour; one rope landward and two towards the sea, where the wind would not toss her about or sun split her or birds of the air befoul her. Then he headed for the nearest pub, "The Dragon's Head," and pointed me in the direction of the coast road.

The road here curves along the coastline, tracing a narrow path between the hills and the sea. The air is clear, and the breeze blows in from the sea, catching the spray and lifting it lightly over the road; I can almost taste the salt on my lips. As I turn past Ballygalley Head, the wind appears to drop; the pedals move faster, the gears become higher, and I suddenly have the sensation of speed and strength. Leaving the shelter of the bay, the illusion is broken; the shoulders begin to strain, thighs tighten, and I slow to an easier pace. Above, the gulls are wheeling with the wind

and the clouds are drifting towards the glens. It is a day of gentle warmth, but when the clouds cover the sun, an unexpected coolness fills the air. In the distance, I can just make out Ailsa Craig off the Scottish coast; it dances in and out of focus, as if willed into existence by an act of imagination.

The road wound past Glenarm and into Carnlough Bay, where I stopped to walk around the harbour and watch the fishing boats being readied for their next journey. "Sweet Carnlough Bay" – the song floated in from the sea:

> When winter was dawning, o'er high hills and mountains
> And dark were the clouds o'er the deep rolling sea
> I spied a fair lass as the daylight was dawning
> She was asking the road to sweet Carnlough Bay.

It has the same tune as "The Road to Dundee," an Antrim version of a Scottish song. But in the Scottish version, the couple who fall in love on the road are forced to follow separate paths; he is of low degree, her father says no, and there is wailing and gnashing of teeth all round, in the true folk tradition. In Carnlough Bay, though, all is sweetness and light. They walk together into town and wind up in Pat Hamill's for a "wee drop," where he drinks to the health of the "dear lassie" he's met. No angst, no agony, no anguish – just a fine time on a warm day.

It's a welcome change from the customary tragic theme. Most Irish love songs worth their salt have at least two suicides, one unwanted pregnancy, and maybe a murder thrown in for good measure; the characters drop like flies, the lovers usually wind up buried side by side, and the last verse generally runs something like:

> Build me a grave, both broad and deep
> A marble tombstone at my feet
> And put these words on the stone above
> To tell the world that I died for love.

The usual pattern would run as follows: he gets her drunk at Pat Hamill's and seduces her on a nearby hillside; she gets pregnant and he disowns her; she drowns herself and he dies of guilt; her parents commit suicide and Pat Hamill goes insane. But we know that this didn't happen in Carnlough Bay; had it done, the balladeer would have added at least another four verses. And balladeers as a breed tend to judge the quality of a song by the quantity of its verses.

"Sweet Carnlough Bay": the song suits the day. Looking around the place, you'd never know it could be otherwise; couples are walking together in the sunshine, and the beach is full of children who are charging into the coldness of the sea, shouting and laughing and shivering, and running themselves back to warmth. The melody is in my mind, but whenever I try to hum it aloud, it eludes me; perhaps the image is illusory as well. I search for Pat Hamill's, but learn that it has long since disappeared. Someone shows me an old photograph of the place, a fine hotel on the main street, with a sign saying "Cyclists Specially Catered For" – Sunday afternoons on old boneshakers, followed by plates of sandwiches and glasses of beer.

Back on the bicycle, I travel on past the short, slumped-back headland of Garron Point, where Cushendall and Cushendun come into view. Across the North Channel, the Mull of Kintyre reaches out from Scotland, bare as a bald head. The sunlight catches the windows of a large white house at Southend, on the edge of the Mull. There used to be a ferry service from Cushendall

to the Mull a few years ago, making the trip in a couple of hours. Now, it takes a couple of days, and the wanderings are well worth the time. You cross over from Larne to Stranraer and travel northwards through the narrow roads of the Scottish coast. Just before Ayr, you pass the Electric Brae, where the Laws of Gravity have been reversed and you find yourself freewheeling up the hill. Further on, you take the ferry to Aran, the island of sharp-edged peaks and soft-eyed deer, until you reach Lochranza. There, in the peace and stillness of the mountain-sheltered bay, you wait for the boat to Kintyre. And you wind your way to Southend, stand by the large white house, and watch the sunset over the Glens of Antrim.

At Garron Point, I took the tin whistle from the pannier, climbed over a fence, sat down on coarse grass, and started to play. A soft tune wafts over the fields, and drifts into the spray of the sea – a piece composed three centuries ago by the blind harper Turlough Carolan for Fanny Power, the daughter of one of his patrons. Then a jig, "Out on the Ocean," skipping over the water, light as a summer's day. The music is made for meandering, and the meandering depends on the mood – the state of your mind, the direction of the wind, the sounds from the sea. A jig or a reel will never sound quite the same way twice; the ornamentations, elaborations, and syncopations will twist and turn through the melody, changing its character as it is played. There is the tune, and there is the way you play the tune; there is the map, and there is the way you choose to travel.

You could race through Ireland in a car, sticking to the main routes; but if you take a bicycle, breathe in the air, and wander off into the side roads, you'd be closer to the spirit of the place. You could learn traditional music by the book, sticking to the main notes; but if you take a tin whistle, breathe out the air, and wander off into the variations, you'd be closer to the spirit of the piece. Riding a bicycle or playing a whistle, the journey becomes more than a means to the end of reaching a destination; it becomes an end in itself, its own destination.

A slow and soothing piece, "The Lark in the Clear Air," hovers over craggy hills; there is melancholy in the melody. In ancient times, the music was said to have magical effects. It could soften the senses and send you to sleep. It could fill the room with laughter, quicken the pulse, set hearts racing. Or it could sadden the soul and move you to weep. And so it still is, from the lightest lullaby, to the liveliest jig, to the loneliest lament. In the tin whistle there is beauty and simplicity, a narrow range of notes and a wide range of feeling. There are slow airs that would make the tears run down your leg, and there are dance tunes that would make your spirits soar. Sometimes, in sessions, the musicians will join them together and move directly from a mournful air to a wild and wonderful set of reels, to banish misfortune with a song.

Time to move on; the tin whistle is tucked back in the pack. Apart from anything else, it's the ideal travel instrument; it's easier to carry on a bicycle than is a guitar, say, or a piano. The whistle is also the ultimate democratic instrument; for the price of a couple of pints (the universal unit of currency for wastrels and minstrels), you can enter the world of jigs and reels, of songs and laments. And as you make the journey, you learn the music by listening to the people who play it, and you soak up the spirit by going to the places where they play it – the kitchens, the pubs, the festivals, in towns and villages all over the country.

Johnny Joe's

I'm heading northwest now, into Red Bay, past half-hidden milestones that click by at five-minute intervals like a cyclist's metronome; four more beats to Johnny Joe's bar in Cushendall. The graffiti tell me that I'm moving into different territory. "Moyle District Council," reads the sign; IRA, INLA, BRITS OUT, say the scratch marks on its surface. This part of the country is a world unto itself; centuries ago, it was part of the Kingdom of Dalriada, reaching out to western Scotland. In late medieval times, it was ruled by the MacDonnell clan, based on the Isle of Islay. Each morning, it is said, the Lord of the Isles would face the east and grant the sun permission to rise over his kingdom. But one day, the sun got tired of his *hubris* and sent King James IV's army from Scotland to knock him off his perch. He and his men flew to the relative safety of remote northern Antrim, where they missed everything, including the Reformation. And that is why, to this day, the area is staunchly Catholic.

The bicycle takes me through Waterfoot and into the village of Cushendall, set back from the sea. I check in to a bed-and-breakfast opposite Johnny Joe's, grab a bite to eat, and cross the street to the pub. It's as well to get there early; there's a session on tonight, and Johnny Joe is unusual among publicans in that he doesn't like his pub to get too full. When he decides that enough is enough, he battens down the hatches, locks his customers in, and keeps the crowds out. All night long, you'll see him guarding the front door – a wiry man somewhere in his seventies, grey stubble on a ruddy face, with his baseball hat and his lumberjack's jacket – peering through the peephole at the people outside and shouting "We're closed! Go away!" whenever the mood takes him.

Gradually, the musicians filter into the lounge, a small room about the size of your average kitchen. The men are in their fifties and sixties; they take their fiddles out of well-worn cases and start to rosin the bows. A woman sits down in front of the piano and gives them the notes. "Did you ever hear an Irishman's definition of foreplay?" asks one of the fiddle players while he's tuning up. "Brace yourself, Bridget!" Then the pianist joins in: "I always thought it was an elbow in the ribs and 'Are ye awake?'" "No, no," says one of her friends; "it's 'Close the curtains.'" A bow is drawn across the strings; they slide into a set of jigs, played at an easy, relaxed pace. The tunes are given time to breathe; the players know what they're about and feel comfortable with their music. There's no reason to hurry; they want to take in the scenery.

Another set of jigs, followed by a set of reels. The room is beginning to fill up; pints of stout are crowding onto the tables. The pianist is laying down bass runs beneath the melodies, the fiddle players are wandering into another world, the doorway into the lounge is jammed with people, and Johnny Joe is patrolling the hall. Suddenly, he locks the front door. This presents something of a problem for me, since

some friends from Whitehead are planning to spend the evening in the Lurig, a pub down the street, and I'd like to visit them. "If I nip out for a few minutes, will you let me back in?" I ask Johnny Joe. "I will not," barks the voice beneath the baseball cap.

I decide to take my chances, open the front door, and narrowly avoid being crushed to death by the inrushing stampede of people. Somewhat shaken, I eventually meet up with my friends. We chat for a couple of pints before they drive back home, leaving me with the task of breaking back in to Johnny Joe's. The queue has subsided; in a kind of Darwinian survival-of-the-fittest process, the aggressive had elbowed their way inside when I'd opened the door to get out, and the passive had decided to drink themselves into the ground at the Cushendall Arms. Only the desperate were left. I stood in front of the peephole, knowing that Johnny Joe was staring out, and tried to charm my way in. No use: "We're closed! Go away!"

But you could hear the music coming from the front room, and it sounded wonderful – something that cast its spell and drew you in. So I climbed up on the windowledge, stretched my head through the horizontal upper window, and began to play the whistle through the opening. "C'mon down," they laughed; "we'll see you're all right." It didn't look promising; even if you could make it through the narrow opening, you still had the problem of getting down from the ceiling to the floor. But Guinness gives you courage, the music was like a magnet, and everyone was shouting encouragement. "I'll give it a try, if you'll let these lads in after me" – the desperate, after all, must stick together. "You're all welcome; c'mon now." Hands hoisted me upwards, I clambered sideways to the opening, and hovered precariously between the world within and the world without.

The only time I'd been in a remotely comparable position was during a drama workshop in northern Ontario run by a mad Italian who kept insisting – with a little too much emphasis – that "this is not Group Therapy." Among other things, he made us stand on the edge of the stage and free-fall backwards to the hall below, where our fellow actors were waiting to catch us. It was an unnerving experience; you wanted to keep looking behind you to make sure they hadn't all wandered off for a cup of tea or a smoke-break or something, but you weren't allowed to turn around – it was supposed to be a "Trust Exercise." As you tilted backwards, you half-expected to split your skull on the hall floor, only to land safely in their outstretched arms. But the actors had been sober and were well coached in the art of catching falling bodies; the folks at Johnny Joe's were paralytic, polluted, and pissed, and were more used to people coming in through the door than the upper window.

It occurred to me that perhaps this wasn't such a good idea after all. But by then it was too late; I could either fall forwards into the pub, or backwards into the street. "C'mon down. D'ye want to be stuck there all night?" they called out. This was the ultimate trust exercise. And down I went, rolling towards the Guinness-packed table and flashing forward to my obituary ("he died in the over-zealous pursuit of truth and beauty, impaled by the very bottles which had given him so much inspiration in life"), when a rush of arms reached out to save me. I became weightless, as a hundred hands guided me into the centre of the room, held me there for a moment, and set me down. Cheers and applause and thanks, as the colour came back to my face and I realized I was still alive. Meanwhile, the next person had already positioned himself for the horizontal roll into the room, and the line-up outside was beginning to grow.

And so it went for the next hour, Johnny Joe out in the hall guarding a locked door, while half of Cushendall came in through the window. Gradually, the musicians picked it up again; a tune called "Oh those britches full of stitches" started off a set of polkas, and a new vitality was in the air. Sessions have their own rhythms, their own ebbs and flows of energy, and this one was beginning to find its pace. The music had taken over; it coursed through the fiddle players, controlled them, made them incapable of stopping. Tune ran into tune, and set ran into set; jigs became hornpipes, hornpipes became reels, and reels turned back into jigs. It seemed to go on for ever, carrying us along on a light wave of euphoria.

Only the desire for Guinness and the call of nature pulled me out of there. In the toilet, you'd sometimes see people standing at the wall with their pint in one hand and their penis in the other, pouring it in and pissing it out simultaneously. "What's the definition of an

Irishman?" runs an old joke. "A complex mechanism for transforming Guinness into urine."

On one of the trips back from the bar to the lounge, weaving my way through crammed corridors, I heard a steady, insistent rapping at the door. Johnny Joe went up to the peephole, his eyes as big as banjos, and began hammering back. "You can turn yourself around," he shouted, "because you're never coming into my pub." The recipient of these remarks was one of the best fiddle players in the district, but also one of the least popular; he had a reputation for arrogance and for borrowing things without asking. Undeterred by Johnny Joe's hostility, and unwilling to take the window route, he kept on knocking and knocking. Johnny Joe, unable to take it any more, opened the door to tell him to his face that he was not welcome – a tactical error if ever there was one. Seeing the opening, the Fiddle Player and his entourage shouldered their way through, brushing Johnny Joe back against the wall. "All right, yous can come in," said Johnny Joe, bowing to the inevitable, "but you're not taking that fiddle out of its case, d'ye hear? You're not spoiling any sessions in my pub." The Fiddle Player didn't deign to reply; he and his friends made it to the bar, bought their drinks, and headed straight to the lounge. The musicians nodded their heads warily, as the intruder took out his fiddle, tuned it a quarter tone above theirs, and started to play like fire. They supped on their pints, started chatting among themselves, and slowly put their instruments away. Technically, the Fiddle Player was better than the rest of them put together; but the magic of the session had been broken.

The following day was a fragile one; the head was heavy, the stomach unsettled, the muscles weary. I kept dropping things. Tasks that used to be straightforward, like tying up shoelaces, expanded into major tests of dexterity. Everything was twice as loud as it should have been. Reading the newspaper was impossible; black lines blurred against a smudged background. There seemed little choice but to declare a Day of Recovery and adjust my movements to the mood. Besides, after the crowded conviviality of Johnny Joe's, I longed for the open spaces and wind-swept silences of the countryside. And so, after nine cups of tea at the local cafe, I slowly made my way westwards to the Glens of Antrim and the neolithic burial site known as Ossian's Grave.

Ossian was the legendary son of the legendary Warrior Hero Fionn mac Cumhaill. In Irish folklore, these larger-than-life characters generally had to prove themselves in a series of quests, which involved such improbable feats as beheading giants, turning themselves into birds or animals, slaying supernatural boars, forcing fiddle players to keep in tune, and such like. The stories are full of fantasy and violence; the heroes are men of courage and honour, Macho Celts who are in it for the glory and the girls, in that order of preference. During the eighteenth century, Ossian was resurrected into a romantic cult figure, the archetypal folk hero who emerged from the mists of antiquity to symbolize ancient Celtic virtues. The Scots tried to claim him as one of their own; a couple of con artists from the Highlands began to circulate forgeries of Ossian's "poems" to prove his Caledonian origins. The poems were insipid; the Irish were incensed. As if by way of revenge, they established a counter-myth that located Ossian's grave in the Antrim hills, within a disdainful giant's spitting distance of the far shore. The Great Celtic Hero, in this version, took one look at Scotland and promptly dropped dead.

The road to the grave winds past hillside farmhouses and fields of grazing sheep. The ogres and the giants have long since departed, most of them slain by a succession of kings and warriors working off excessive testosterone levels. All that remains is a deranged dog, baring its teeth, bristling its back, and blocking the path that leads to Ossian. And if it was a dog, it was the most ferocious, most fanatical, most frightening dog you would ever meet; you could see the whole world beneath his legs, and nothing at all between his head and the sky. And if I was a warrior, we would have fought for seven days and seven nights, making the hard places soft and the soft places hard, squeezing the marrow from each other's bones, flooding the valleys with our blood. But I am a New Age, not a

Stone Age, Celt. I realize that the dog's reactions are valid in terms of his experience, that he is only responding to instinctive territorial imperatives, and that he is very much in touch with his own anger. Besides, he'd probably bite my legs off. So, I edge my way past him, whisper softly to his Inner Puppy, and slide past to the side of safety.

Up the hill, beyond the reaches of Canine the Barbarian, the gravestones are scattered in a remote field, amid tufts of rough green grass. I catch the scent of gorse on the breeze, the incense of spring. But thirty centuries of earth press down on the tough, scrawny, wiry people who once walked these hills and fought a bare and brutal struggle for survival in the face of muck and rain and lice and disease, only to become resurrected as Giant Heroes, Warrior Kings, Ossianic Supermen.

Lingering on this lost world beneath my feet, I slowly returned to the road and walked back down to Cushendall, with its peat fires and warm homes and paved roads and electric lights and televisions and telephones and churches and cemeteries. But after nine more cups of tea, the hangover still lay heavy on the head. To soothe the senses, I walked to Tiveragh Hill, the place where the fairies lived; early in the morning, before the humans awoke, they would emerge from the slopes and play hurley on the hillside. I travelled on to Lurig Mountain, where the farms reach upwards to the line of cultivation, the point at which order can no longer impose itself on wilderness. In the park below, the human hurlers were cracking sticks against the ball, fighting it out for supremacy, playing roughly by the rules on a carefully marked-out pitch. I followed the road down the River Dall, beyond their receding shouts, past the well-groomed golf course with its sandtraps to the coarse-grained beach with its clumps of wild grass.

"What're you doin' here, then?" The voice came from nowhere, as if it had been thrown up from the sea. Turning around, I saw three of them – skinny, mean, angular, with narrow eyes and crooked teeth – moving towards me, challenging, menacing. Behind them were the rest of the gang, vandalizing a disused beach hut, looking for something else to hit. "Just passing the time," I said, trying to sound casual and not succeeding. They didn't like my accent. "He's a fuckin' Brit," one said to another. And then to me: "Where do you come from? Are you a Catholic or Protestant or what?" An escape route – an "or what" category. I moved into it as quickly as I could. "I'm from Canada," I said; "we don't have Protestants and Catholics there." "We thought you was a fuckin' Brit," came the reply. "You'd be fuckin' dead if you was a fuckin' Brit. s.a.s. Stripped and Shot."

"Where are you from yourselves?" I asked, trying to get out of their spotlight. "Bawnmore," they said – Bawnmore, an embattled housing estate on the northern edge of Belfast, full of gangs and graffiti, knife-edged next to the overwhelmingly Loyalist estate of Rathcoole; Bawnmore, with its hardmen and its hijackers, its underworld and its unemployment. "We're the Bawnmore Zulus." They'd seen a film on tv about the Zulus and liked their chant – zu-lu, zu-lu. "Chucky Ar La, We're inla," shouted another; Tiocfaidh Ár Lá, Our Day Will Come, the Irish National Liberation Army. The inla was a splinter group from the ira, with something of a reputation for attracting psychopaths; I don't think these lads were actually members, but their sympathies were clear. They told me about "brickin' the Brits," and petrol-bombing the police and army patrols that invaded their territory. I'd seen it on tv, I said. "Yeah, but you never see what they do to us – firin' plastics, callin' us shite, liftin' us at three in the morning. You never see that. Come up to Bawnmore and see for yourself; we'll show you. You can stay at our house, if you want."

From the beach hut behind them, their mates called out to find out what was going on. "It's all right, he's on our side," they called back. I wasn't a clearly defined enemy, I'd listened to their side of the story, and I hadn't challenged what they said; therefore, I was one of them. I was stranded between sea and land, sounding like an ally to avoid being a target. Whatever you say, you say nothing; let the folks at Hooks's Bar think you're Church of Ireland, let the Bawnmore Zulus think you're a Republican, keep your head down, keep quiet, survive.

I turned to go. "Safe home, now," they said. "The Bawnmore Zulus; we'll see you right. Chucky Ar La!" They moved back to their mates and picked up where they'd left off, beating up the dilapidated boards of a broken-down hut. I walked back up the road, past the golf course, towards well-kept houses and peat fires, safe, silent, afraid.

The Skerry Inn

The next day, I decided to make my way to Newtown Crommelin, in the Glens of Antrim, for a session at the Skerry Inn. Unsure of the route, I stopped in at one of the local pubs for directions and started a debate that drew in half the town. "Newtown Crommelin, is it?" said Jimmy MacDonnell, propping himself up against the bar. "It would be easier to find your way to Moscow than Newtown Crommelin. Just get on a plane that's going to Moscow and there you are. But Newtown Crommelin? That's a different matter altogether." His friend, Bob Bradshaw, started to draw a map, which met with a collective shaking of heads and murmurs of discontent; the confusion was as thick as the cigarette smoke.

Eventually, the barman tried to take charge. "Look, take no notice of them," he said; "I'll show you the way." I nodded appreciatively and began to scribble down his instructions. "All right. You take the main road out of town. Then you come to a crossroads. There's a steep hill coming down from the right, and there's a petrol station on the left. And you'll see a farmhouse about fifty yards down the road to your left. Ignore them all and go straight ahead. Then you bear right after taking a fork to the left and going past the wee shop just beyond the white building on your right ..." By the time he'd finished, I had three pages of notes and was totally perplexed; Moscow was looking better and better by the minute. "How're you gettin' there, anyway?" asked the barman. "On a bicycle," I answered. "Jesus, you're fuckin' cracked," was the instant and unanimous verdict. "For Chrissake, catch yourself on," said Jimmy MacDonnell; "look, I'll drive you there myself."

It was a generous offer and I accepted. We had a bite to eat, a thick brown stew suggested by the barman. "What's in it?" I inquired, foolishly. "Oh, he was a grand wee animal," came the reply; "you should've seen the way he ran about the place, barking and wagging his tail." "Such beautiful big puppy-dog eyes, too," added Jimmy. "And that would be called Irish Stew, would it?" I asked with mock innocence, trying to up the ante. "Aye, that's what they call it in most places," the barman shot back. "But round here, it's called Irish Setter."

On the way to the Skerry Inn, we stopped to pick up Archie, an imp of a man who had been singing in the sessions for years. When he saw the car coming, he leapt lightly down from the wooden gate

where he'd been waiting for a ride and greeted us with a lively "Hie! How are you?" To celebrate his good fortune, he entertained us on the journey with "Master McGrath," a nineteenth-century ballad about a champion Irish greyhound who defeated the best racing dogs England had to offer and rubbed it in by shouting "Long live the Republic!" when he crossed the finishing line.

"Which d'ye prefer?" he asked me when he had finished; "jigs or reels?" This began a long and lively discussion about the different forms of traditional music. The jigs have deeper Irish roots; they stretch back several centuries, and probably emerged from the clan marches of old. They are in 6/8 time and jog along at a light-hearted pace, with a happy-go-lucky, slightly mischievous spirit. The reels are more recent; they came in from Scotland towards the end of the eighteenth century, and were immediately and enthusiastically embraced by Irish musicians. They are in 4/4 time and belt along at a speed that would do credit to Master McGrath himself; they have a wild, frenetic feel, and are as close as you can get to ethnic rock and roll. Which did I prefer? It all depended on how I was feeling, I said, and that might change from day to day. Archie would have none of it. "Give me a good reel, every time," he said; "there's nothing like dancing to a good set of reels."

As he spoke, you could almost swear that you were listening to a Scottish accent; visitors from Scotland sometimes think that the Antrim Coasters are sending them up with bad imitations of an Ayrshire dialect. Still, Archie had his own distinct expressions, like the attention-grabbing "Hie!" which prefaced almost everything he said, and the all-purpose "now that's a tragedy" which he used to describe any kind of misfortune, from a broken string to a broken heart. "Why did you never get married, Archie?" a fellow passenger asked him. "Hie! Now that's a tragedy," he said; "that's a tragedy in my life." And he went straight into another song, about the "'Oul Lamass Fair in Ballycastle'O." "Hie! It'll be a grand night tonight," he said as the car pulled into Newtown Crommelin. The reels would breathe life into weary bones; the tragedies could take care of themselves.

We were early; the only person in the pub was an Old-Grey-Fellow lodged in front of the fire, with a dusty old dog at his feet;

they looked like permanent fixtures. I joined him for a chat, leaning forward from the edge of the seat to catch his soft-spoken words and decipher his near-impenetrable accent. He used to be a shepherd, he told me, walking through the Glens with his dog, his collar up against the wind and the rain. He would while away the hours by reciting ballads that he learned when he was a boy, before he was set to work minding sheep. "I still tell them to myself in my head, you know," he said. He cradled his whiskey and moved easily into the metres of Tennyson and Longfellow – poems which had been drilled into him by some nineteenth-century schoolteacher, which had sustained him out on the hills, and which he had brought down into the bar for company, as he waited for the evening to come to life around him.

It would not be long now; people were drifting in, ordering up their pints, and catching up on the news. The long table by the window was set aside for the musicians, who gradually gathered around with their instruments. There was Alec with his four-string banjo, beside Eileen and Liz with their fiddles; next to them sat Dominic, another fiddle player, a man with a kind face and gentle eyes. Further along, there was a fragile-looking fellow in his eighties, bent double over his mandolin; beyond him were two serious-looking accordion players, providing the heavy artillery of the session. At the end of the table, with her back to the others, Mary sat at the piano, ready to play the melodies

and the rhythmical accompaniment of bass runs for the tunes. And around the other side, there was John with his whistle and a set of bones that he would click together at rapid-fire pace when he wanted to send the music into overdrive. The circle was completed by two more fiddle players, one of whom was visiting from southern Ontario; they tuned their instruments, wet their whistles, and steadied themselves for the night's playing.

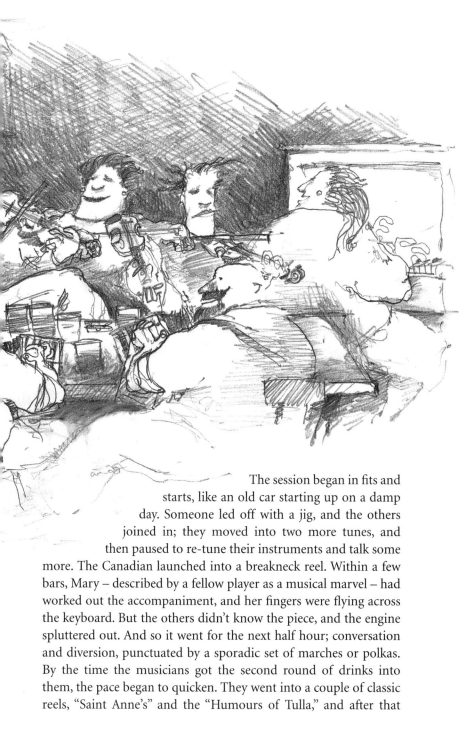

The session began in fits and
starts, like an old car starting up on a damp
day. Someone led off with a jig, and the others
joined in; they moved into two more tunes, and
then paused to re-tune their instruments and talk some
more. The Canadian launched into a breakneck reel. Within a few
bars, Mary – described by a fellow player as a musical marvel – had
worked out the accompaniment, and her fingers were flying across
the keyboard. But the others didn't know the piece, and the engine
spluttered out. And so it went for the next half hour; conversation
and diversion, punctuated by a sporadic set of marches or polkas.
By the time the musicians got the second round of drinks into
them, the pace began to quicken. They went into a couple of classic
reels, "Saint Anne's" and the "Humours of Tulla," and after that

they were away. A tune called "The Boys from Blue Hill" announced a set of hornpipes, which was followed by "The Lark in the Morning" and a series of jigs. The space between sets became shorter and shorter, and the speed of the tunes started to pick up; the musicians were drawing on each other's energy and creating new currents of electricity.

This was in no sense a performance; they were playing for themselves, not for the people around them. Performers appear on a stage; the musicians were grouped around a table, and at least half of them had their backs to the bar. Performers demand an audience; the musicians rode on a wave of noise and laughter. Anything here approaching respectful silence would probably have scared them into stopping. Some people were standing next to the session, watching and listening, but most were sitting around their own tables and sharing stories with their friends, in their own circles. At the end of a set of tunes, nobody clapped; applause would have been incongruous, a source of mild embarrassment.

The music was played in a magic ring, with its own inner secrets and hidden rituals. Within the circle, the musicians would rarely discuss the tunes they were about to play; instead, one of them would provide the cues by starting a jig or a reel, and the others would join in. Through a nod or a glance, through years of acquired understandings, they would slide from one set of tunes to another, easily and effortlessly. Dominic, the fiddle player, initially got things rolling; Alec on the banjo took over for a while, and then one of the accordionists provided the lead – and when an accordionist leads, the others have no choice but to follow. Just as the tunes began in a more-or-less spontaneous way, they would generally finish without a flourish. In contrast to performance music, the last few notes would usually be thrown away; the musicians had said what they wanted to say, the tunes had run their course, and the magic in the ring was momentarily broken.

The closest I'd come to this kind of thing in North America was at a festival of Old Time music in western Virginia. There were fiddles and five-string banjos, mandolins, guitars, and stand-up basses; the sound lay somewhere between traditional Irish music and modern bluegrass. The magic circles of musicians were formed around campfires, under an expanse of stars, rather than in crowded, dense-pack pubs. As in Ireland, the music was fuelled by alcohol; but instead of Guinness, it was a concoction called Henry McKenna's Kentucky Sour Mash Bourbon, which was passed liberally from mouth to mouth – not quite as smooth, but equally effective. In Ireland, the musicians would rarely play the same tune more than twice, and would string several jigs or reels together before shifting gear and moving into a new set; depending on the energy level, they might play continuously for an hour or more. But in Virginia, they would spend several minutes deciding which piece to play, and would then repeat it over and over again, until they ran out of steam. The Virginian tunes had bizarre titles, which often served as refrains in the middle of the melody; you might be focusing on some fast and furious fiddle playing, when suddenly all the musicians would break into a chant of "Nail That Catfish to the Tree." There was no equivalent of that in Ireland; you reached for more of the Sour Mash to steady your nerves.

Guinnesses jostled with whiskey glasses for space on Skerry Inn tables, as the magic ring expanded to embrace more musicians and pulsed its rhythms through the room. After a whirl of reels, the session finally span to a standstill, leaving space for singing. "Let's have some order, ladies and gentlemen," called PJ, the Master of Ceremonies; we were about to move into the performance phase of the evening. "There's someone here tonight who's come all the way from Scotland," he continued. "Would you give us a song, love?" A young woman with frizzy brown hair and roll-your-own cigarettes nodded her assent and started to sing:

> Oh the summer time is coming
> And the leaves are sweetly blooming
> And the wild mountain thyme
> Blows around the purple heather
> Will ye go, lassie, go?

A soft voice carried through the stillness, over glasses and ashtrays, past half-closed eyes and easy smiles. And when she came to the chorus, she was enfolded in harmony, brought back from performance to participation:

> And we'll all go together
> Where the wild mountain thyme
> Blows around the purple heather
> Will ye go, lassie, go?

"Well now, that was very good, very good indeed," said PJ when it was over. "And that was very good order, ladies and gentlemen. Why don't you give us another one?" She didn't know any more traditional songs, she said; would it be all right if she did something else? "Your pleasure, love; your pleasure." So she moved into George Gershwin's "Summertime," curling the sounds of jazz and blues through smoke-filled air. Approval and applause; traditional or modern, a good singer was a good singer. "Well now," commented PJ, "it isn't often that we get to hear blues in the Skerry Inn. Very good, very good indeed."

That set the pattern for the rest of the night's songs. PJ would call for silence, invite someone to sing, congratulate the audience for its order and the singer for the song, ask for an encore, and move on to the next person. Lawrence was up next, a traditional singer who embroidered his melodies with intricate ornamental patterns. The ornamentations became an integral part of the songs, in much the same way that the embellishments in a jig or a reel became part of the tunes themselves. Like all good traditional singers, Lawrence recreated a song each time he sang it; he was inseparable from the song, just as the session musicians were inseparable from their tunes.

After that, the mixture of melodies became increasingly eclectic. A woman who had smoked too many cigarettes sang a couple of songs about unrequited love and the pain of parting; it was as close as you could get to traditional Irish hurtin' music. Then there were some sentimental nineteenth-century music hall pieces, followed by old standards like the "Rose of Mooncoin" and "Mary of Dungloe." Archie, all wires and nerves, had his fifteen minutes of fame, and then a young lad with a guitar gave us a couple of Christy

Moore songs. Joe Doran, the frail-fingered old fellow with the mandolin, took his turn, hands shaking as he reached for his glass in search of inspiration. But his voice was clear and young – a soft tenor, crooning "John O'Dreams" to a Tchaikovsky tune:

> Home is rover, his journey over,
> Yield up the night time to old John O'Dreams.

When I returned to the Skerry Inn many months later, his chair was empty.

"Well now, that was very good, very good indeed," PJ's voice broke in over the applause. "That was very good order, ladies and gentlemen; thank you very much indeed. And now, let's get back to the music" – as if we'd just been listening to something different altogether. The noise level gradually rose, the players checked their tunings, and resumed with a set of reels, almost knocking Archie off his chair. I got up for more Guinness and fell instantly in love with the maid behind the bar. "It must be great working here and hearing all this music," I said as she pulled the pint. "To tell you the truth," she replied, "I don't really like this diddly-i-di music at all. In fact, I can't stand it; it all sounds the same to me." A bucket of cold water over the head. Still, her verdict wasn't as bad as that of a Protestant woman I'd met earlier on my travels: "Whining Catholic Music," she'd called it, in a whining voice of her own.

Nothing could have been further from the truth; the music was exciting and enchanting, as clear an affirmation of life as you could find. Alec and Eileen invited me to join the musicians' table, and I sat with my pint and my whistle, waiting for a tune I knew to come round. They had a seemingly inexhaustible repertoire; I could play perhaps one tune in ten and felt like a bit of a fraud. But they didn't mind, and offered smiles of encouragement whenever I joined in. Except in the upper register, the whistle tends to get drowned out by the other instruments in a session. This can be a problem for accomplished players; as someone said to me, you could just as easily be blowing on a candle for all the difference it makes. For a relative beginner like me, though, it has its advantages; the mistakes are not glaringly obvious, and the combined volume of the other instruments acts as a kind of musical safety-net. It's a good way to learn, playing with people who are open and friendly, and knowing that you can't do too much damage to the music.

Closing time came and closing time went, happily ignored by everyone. "When do you stop serving drinks?" I asked the barman shortly after eleven. "October," he replied. This was a slight exaggeration; the place dried up and the musicians wound down somewhere between two and three in the morning. But then we were invited into the kitchen for gallons of tea and dozens of sandwiches – a Skerry Inn thank you to the musicians, and an antidote of sorts for the alcohol. There would be some bleary eyes the next morning; PJ would be teaching mathematics at a local secondary school, Alec would be working as a motor parts salesman, and I would be struggling along the road to Ballycastle. But we would all have the music ringing in our ears.

The High Part of the Road

As you leave Cushendall, you have a choice between two routes. The main road leads you along the Dall River and up into the glens, through a wilderness of heather, towards the dark and mysterious Loughareema, the Vanishing Lake of the hills. On a dry day, all you will see is a mud-encrusted valley; but when it rains, as it has been known to do, the water level rises suddenly and sharply. Back in 1888, before high walls were put up to protect the road, an entire carriage, complete with a colonel, coachman, and two horses, was swallowed up by the lake on a storm-swept night. "Drive on to hell," the colonel had instructed the coachman, and that's precisely what the coachman did; it was the last act of obedience in his life.

The other road is a narrow track that climbs directly over the coastal mountains and keeps you as close as possible to the sea – and this was the road I decided to take. My new-found friends in Cushendall thought I was mad, and may well have been right. "You *can't* cycle on that road," one said; "nobody can. You'll wind up walking up all the hills and freewheeling down them; you'll never even turn your pedals." This might have been true for the traditional three-speed bicycle, but certainly not for the high-tech multigeared modern mountain bike; with one of those, you'd only walk up half the hills. After a vertical takeoff from Cushendall, the road passes by the old Layd Church, where you can rest in the ruins and inspect the gravestones – the MacDonnell clan, unknown sailors who never made it through the North Channel, unknown cyclists who never made it up the hill. Then it climbs past herds of cattle being walked to new pastures, and up beyond the livestock line. Looking back, there's a magnificent view of Red Bay, the Lurig Mountain overlooking Cushendall, and Tiveragh Hill, where distant figures with hurley sticks can faintly be seen in the morning light. Eventually, the road levels out and drops down steeply to sea level at the town of Cushendun.

Here, you can walk along a quiet beach past houses that look as though they come from Cornwall, and make your way to the concealed caves that carve through the cliffs at the south end of the bay. I stopped for much-needed refreshments at the Cushendun Hotel, run by Randal the Polymath – publican, veterinarian, town councillor, biker, and eccentric. There are no clearly defined hours at the Cushendun Hotel; Randal opens it when he feels like it and closes it when he feels like it, no matter who is there or what they're doing. On the walls, the Rules of the Bar, in the form of Messages of Doom, stare down at the customers: BUSHMILLS MAKES YOU CARNAPTIOUS, DRINK DESTROYS YOUR LIVER, and, in case you think that the words he had spoken were only in jest, I MEAN THIS – unorthodox sentiments for a publican.

Having dutifully avoided anything remotely alcoholic, I set out for the second leg of the day's journey, from Cushendun to Ballycastle. Leaving the village, I immediately encountered another Message of Doom: ROAD UNSUITABLE FOR CARAVANS, or, translated into Cyclespeak, ROAD IMPOSSIBLE FOR BICYCLES. But if it's one of the most back-breaking climbs in the country, it's also one of the most beautiful. Below the hills, a thin white layer of mist covered the channel, making you feel higher than the clouds, yet close to the sea. It was a day of magic and mirages, a day without edges, when nothing was sharply defined or clearly delineated. The Mull of Kintyre loomed through the haze and seemed to be suspended over the horizon. High over the hillside to my left a skylark was singing, trilling intricate patterns of notes like the ornamentations on a whistle. I sat by the road and played the soft, wistful air of "Eleanor Plunkett" to the birds and the sea and the mist, and let the tune melt into the day, into the bleeting of lambs and the bellowing of cows, into the wind-wafted smell of gorse and manure, into the land of weather-beaten sheep and stone fences, into the stillness, into itself.

Legs push, heart pumps, pedals turn slowly up the slopes; on the hills above, a hare in the heather darts into the distance. Round a corner, Torr Head suddenly comes into view, jutting out towards Scotland. Sheer cliffs cut into the sea, the smoke of burning gorse curls over the hillside, and the eastern side of Rathlin Island appears in the sea-mist. Ahead, the road is corkscrewing higher and higher, in curves of excruciating steepness. I turn off to Torr Head, letting the bicycle race down to the sea, past the shell of a mansion and an abandoned coastguard station. It is completely deserted; no cars, no people, definitely no caravans, nothing. The place has a lonely, wild, eerie feel to it; I sit on rough, unkempt grass and stare out to sea, feeling like the last person left on Earth.

The road back to the world is steep and tough and hard and long; gears and knees creak and strain at the pressure, and the wheels wobble the bike from one side of the road to the other. Stubbornly, stupidly, I keep pushing forward, concentrating every ounce of energy from long training sessions back in Toronto. You have to be fit for this kind of thing; to prepare myself, I spent many hours at the local athletic centre, tied to a stationary bicycle, breathing in fumes of stale sweat and chlorine. In front of me were disco-driven aerobics classes, where women in skin-tight petroleum-based out-fits did push-ups and sit-ups and jumping jacks; to the side were the weight machines and mirrors, where muscle-bound men grunted and groaned like monosyllabic cavemen. If gender differ-ences are socially conditioned, the conditioners should be very proud of themselves. "Three more, two more, one more," shouted the aerobics instructor; "three more, two more, one more," I told my legs on the Torr Head road, before they ground themselves to a halt. Eighteen gears on the bike, eighteen weeks of hard training, and still I could not make it up this hill. There was no choice: I walked the rest of the way, my heart pounding like a steam-hammer, until the gradient levelled out from an eighty-degree to a sixty-degree angle. And then I collapsed by the side of the road, drained of energy, a shell of my former self.

Eventually, the pulse rate returned to something approaching normal, I reluctantly heaved myself back on the bicycle, and strug-gled onwards to Murlough Bay. Exhaustion and euphoria; half way down the spiral path to the shore, beside the fierce cliffs of Fair Head, I stretched myself out between the earth and the Sun. Nearby, a sheep was slowly munching the grass; one of her lambs lay quietly on the ground, while the other lazily washed itself. Above, two birds were singing messages to each other; in the distance, a cuckoo was calling. Somewhere in the haze between Fair Head and the Mull of Kintyre, a ship was passing through the North Channel; it seemed to be suspended between sea and sky, sailing through the clouds. "The Ship in the Clouds" – it's the name of an old-time fiddle tune, an optical illusion set to music. The melody runs through my mind and gradually gives me the energy to walk down to the bay and wander through the ruins of Drumnakill Church, where a small flock of people worshipped beneath the shelter of Fair Head more than a thousand years ago and sustained themselves from the sea.

Back on the high part of the road, you can walk across the moorland to the top of Fair Head, until the land disappears into the sea with heart-stopping suddenness. Here, on the edge of existence, strange and unpredictable cliff creatures have made their home – gruagaigh and elves, jokers in the pack. They will help you if they choose, but they will hurt you if you cross them. A gruagach might assist an old and ailing farmer in threshing his corn; but if the farmer leaves out bread and milk by way of thanks, the gruagach, realizing that his presence has been detected, will never return. If you come too close to the elves, they will pelt you with magic stones; you could be sure that cattle with lumps under their skin had been hit by elfshot, and it would be touch and go whether they would live.

Like the fairies of Islandmagee, the gruagaigh and elves live in magic rings around thorn bushes, and ill fortune will fall on anyone who disturbs them. A Fair Head farmer once cut a branch from a thorn bush to clear a path for his horses as they ploughed the field. The next day, he noticed that one of his cows had its tail missing; it was eventually found hanging on the bush, in the very place where the branch had been. Worse luck followed; when he went to the smithy the next day to sharpen his ploughshare, a spark leapt up from the forge and blinded him in one eye. God only knows what would have happened to him had he pulled the whole bush down. At any rate, cyclists who want to avoid punctures or worse would be well advised to steer clear of the thorn bushes around Fair Head, just to be on the safe side.

Leaving the land of gruagaigh and elves, I cycled down to Ballycastle, past the golf course and tennis courts and amusement arcades, where the people of the otherworld never venture. After settling in at a bed-and-breakfast, I let the sea cool my feet and walked through rockpools and gentle waves towards the community of Corrymeela, just up the coast. Corrymeela was set up during the early years of the Troubles, as an interdenominational antidote to the political and religious poison of the North. The community brings Protestant and Catholic children together for holidays, and is part of a broader movement to break down the stereotypes that each side holds about the other, and to build some degree of understanding and compassion across the divide. In a society where some ministers spout off about a Popish conspiracy to take over the world, and some priests are secretly sympathetic to the IRA, Corrymeela represents the better side of religion in the province. It is a voice of hope in a political wilderness.

The volunteer workers showed me around the ground, with its recreation areas and its chapel that accommodates both Protestant and Catholic services – no mean feat in theologically correct Northern Ireland. They introduced me to John Morrow, a Presbyterian minister and peace activist who was one of the founders of the community, and we talked over a pot of tea. I asked him how much difference he thought groups like Corrymeela could really make, how they could start rolling back four hundred years of hatred. "There isn't any kind of instant answer to this situation," he said. "What you've got to do is have a very long perspective, realizing that at times forces are working against you that are destroying a lot of your work, but believing that at the same time a lot of other things are real seeds that are being planted, some of which you can see are beginning to germinate. Things like support groups for partners in mixed Catholic-Protestant marriages, groups to help young people caught up in paramilitary organizations, groups for ex-prisoners, groups for the bereaved. And just, above all, new relationships where at least a significant minority of people are learning to work together in new ways and with real trust, but with a realistic awareness of their differences."

I admire him and everything he stands for, but I still have to fight off a tidal wave of scepticism. I remember the comment of a Sinn Féin supporter I met in a North Antrim pub: "Of course Protestants and Catholics can get on together well as people," she had said; "everybody knows that. The question is, do they think that the state of Northern Ireland should exist, or that it should cease to exist?" Put like that, it seems very stark; and something tells me that she is probably right. But maybe, just maybe, the work of John Morrow and Corrymeela might make things a little less stark, might widen the middle ground, might move us away from the dichotomies and might even change the terms of the question. Maybe, maybe not. If the future should belong to anybody, it should belong to them.

Back in Ballycastle, the evening was stirring into life and the pubs were beginning to fill with laughter. The musicians were meeting at McCarroll's pub for their regular Thursday night session; they played in a large wooden shed at the back, which they nicknamed the Hen House; appropriately enough, the first tune of the evening was a reel called "Jenny's Chickens." Dominic from the Skerry Inn was there, along with Leo on the accordion and Billy McKee on the fiddle – a tall, balding man in his late sixties who played with his eyes shut, lost in the fire and passion of his music. They were joined by a fiddle player from Scotland and his German wife, who brought along her harp; the two of them had recently moved into the area to live by the sea and soak up the sessions. Dominic and Leo took the lead – and there isn't a tune composed that Dominic doesn't know. Feet tapped on the floor; drinks vibrated in glasses; Billy came close to losing his whiskey as it rattled slowly down to the table's edge; the music reverberated through the room and filled the courtyard outside, drawing more and more people towards it.

Among them was a very large and very drunk woman from Glasgow, on a fortnight's holiday in Ballycastle. "Where's the man with the wee drum?" she called out repeatedly; "I want the man with the wee drum." The man in question was a genial fellow by the name of George; the "wee drum" was the bodhrán, or goatskin drum, which she had heard him play the week before. She was only there for the banging of the drum, George hadn't arrived yet, it was ten o'clock already, and she was losing patience; her voice became higher as the whiskey in her glass became lower. The only purpose of the other instruments, she was convinced, was to provide an accompaniment for the bodhrán player – an approach that more than a few bodhrán players have been known fully to endorse, much to the chagrin of their back-up bands. "What's the best way to play the bodhrán?" someone once asked Seamus Ennis, one of Ireland's greatest traditional musicians. "With a penknife," he replied.

George and his bodhrán finally showed up half an hour later. Seamus Ennis notwithstanding, he played it well, matching the rhythmic phrasing of the other musicians and achieving a kind of subliminal effect; you only noticed the bodhrán when it wasn't actually there. But this wasn't good enough for the Glaswegian, who hadn't been waiting all night for something that didn't seem to be there. "Play it louder, play it louder," she yelled out to George, full throttle. "He doesn't play it loud enough," she said to me in an aside, just in case I'd missed her point; I began checking my back-pack for a penknife. And then to George: "For cripe's sake, man, don't be afraid of the bloody thing; give it here!" She wrenched the bodhrán from his hands and began to bang on the wee drum for all she was worth. It was loud. It was very loud indeed. It had all the subtlety of a sledgehammer hitting a fencepost.

George looked mildly bemused. The other musicians tried to salvage the situation by turning from reels and jigs to slow airs, on the normally safe assumption that it's impossible to accompany a slow air on the bodhrán. Unfortunately, this musical nuance was lost on the Glaswegian, who continued to bang away happily in a rhythm that increasingly came to resemble the Morse Code. To save their souls, the musicians put their instruments down, headed for the bar, and ordered several whiskeys apiece. Meanwhile, the Glaswegian and her teenage son began to pose for photographs with the bodhrán and George; he looked, and probably felt, like a dog being washed. The barman passed two large plates of sandwiches around the musicians' table, the chat turned to horses and how to look after them, George eventually got his bodhrán back, and the session gradually resumed. The Glaswegian was last seen – and heard – in the corner of the courtyard, singing "Glasgow Belongs to Me" at the top of her lungs.

The next day, I decided to give myself a break from the bicycle and took the boat out to Rathlin Island, where the spray of the salt sweeps over the heather. There are no trees and no hedges here; the moors open out to the sea, above the cliffs and caves where the red-capped puffins nest. It was in these caves, some seven centuries ago, that the Scottish warrior Robert the Bruce sheltered from his enemies, watched a spider's repeated efforts to crawl up the walls, and drew the lesson that if at first you don't succeed, you must try and try again. Thus inspired, he returned to Scotland, rallied his men, defeated the Sassenach invaders, and generally became a Great Hero. It is not recorded what happened to the spider.

Life on the island could be hard; there were shortages of fuel, the cattle were said to look like walking shadows, and food supplies had to be rowed in from the mainland. But there was a thriving smuggling trade in whiskey and brandy, along with the local poteen stills, and there were dances and music that lasted through the night; if you missed the last boat to Ballycastle, you would probably die smiling. And the islanders were very practical in a skewed kind of way. For one thing, they would never put more than one family member at a time on the same boat, on the assumption that the family as a whole would have a greater chance of survival. I'm not sure if this is statistically sound, but I see the point; I know people who feel the same way about airplane travel. For another, they refused to learn how to swim, on the assumption that if you fell overboard it would be better to drown sooner rather than later.

Things have changed now, of course; you cross over on a motor boat rather than a rowing boat, and if you can't swim you can always wear a lifejacket. As the boat takes you back to Ballycastle, the north Antrim coast stretches out before you; Knocklayd Mountain towering over the town, the Grey Man's path leading down to the sea at Fair Head, and Benbane Head before the Giant's Causeway to the west. The song of Rathlin Island comes to mind, and stays with me through the crossing:

Sailing southward from Rathlin Island
Past Fair Head and by Murlough Bay
With the north wind to drive us onward
What care we for the wind and spray?

It's a gentle melody, a song of going home, where a day's fishing winds up with a pint or two at McBride's Pub – no great message or meaning, just a feeling of contentment after a good day's work.

Instead of McBride's, I wound up that evening at the House of MacDonnell, another of Ballycastle's session pubs. In the corner of a back room, four lads were playing a fast and furious mixture of reels and jigs – another of those ubiquitous fiddlers, a bodhrán player who had so far escaped the attention of mad tub-thumping Glaswegian women, a guitarist who punched out the rhythm by changing chords at rapid-fire pace, and an uilleann piper who was in constant overdrive, belting out the tunes for all he was worth. The uilleann pipes stick out all over the place; there are drones that underpin the melody, regulators that provide harmonic accompaniment, and a chanter for the tunes themselves; the piper looks as

if he has strapped a pig and an octopus around his body, with the legs and tentacles pointing in all directions at once. Unlike the Scottish bagpipes, which require cheek-bursting blasts of wind into the airbag, the uilleann pipes are powered by bellows that are worked from the elbow; hence the name uilleann, which is Irish for elbow. The sound is softer and sweeter than that of the bagpipes; the uilleann pipes will not drown out every other instrument within a seven-mile radius, and it is possible to spend more than thirty seconds listening to them in a small room without permanently damaging your eardrums.

"That thing must be difficult to play," said an Australian from the Youth Hostel down the road. The piper smiled back; he was in his mid-twenties, with a cloth cap, waist-long hair, and teeth like Stonehenge – a monument to Irish dentistry. "How long have you been playing?" asked the Australian, whose own teeth were perfect. "About two weeks," interjected the fiddle player, grinning from ear to ear. The uilleann pipes are among the hardest traditional instruments to master; they require years of disciplined practice, patience, and determination, as well as a finely developed musical sense. Most pipers begin with the tin whistle when they are kids, and move on to the pipes in their early teens. The pipes either become an obsession, or lie neglected in the corner of the room; there seems to be no middle way with them. The traditional apprenticeship lasts fourteen years; there are seven years of practising, when you work out the fingering and the techniques of ornamentation, followed by seven years of playing, when you learn the tunes and build up your repertoire. Then you are ready to stroll into a pub, strap yourself in, and send the session soaring into the stratosphere. The uilleann piper in the House of MacDonnell had put so much effort into his playing that he made it seem effortless.

In the morning, I cleared my head with a walk beneath the cliffs of Ballycastle and breathed in the clear air of a fresh breeze before starting the day's ride along the Causeway coast. The hills don't seem so steep now, after the grinding gradients of Torr Head, but they're still no pushover. Shortly out of town, the road winds down to Larry Bane Bay, where the Carrick-a-Rede rope bridge swings across to a small island and carries the salmon fishermen to their catches. Two narrow planks are strung together and balanced with side ropes that are supposed to stop you from falling. As you venture across, you hear the whirlpool of water rushing on the rocks some eighty feet below; meanwhile, the bridge moves with the wind and sways with each step. I began to feel whirlpools in my stomach. By the time I reached the middle, all my certainties had disappeared beneath my feet; I longed for the security of solid ground and simple answers, to be walking firmly on one side or the other. My fear of heights threatened to paralyse me; I was suspended on a swaying bridge, caught between the mainland and the island, confused.

Step by step, not daring to look down, I eventually crossed over and back. Two fishermen came by, carrying sacks of salmon; they strode across the bridge as easily as if they were walking down a country lane on a sunny afternoon. But there have been occasions when people froze with fear and were eventually lifted off by helicopter. And this is the place that the Lost Souls claim to cross each year by motorbike; either they have a collective deathwish, or they're simply making the whole thing up. I'd like to think it was the latter, but fear it's the former: "Better to pass boldly into that other world," Deadman would have said, "than fade and wither dismally with age."

After Carrick-a-Rede, the road follows the coastline to Ballintoy and rises over White Park Bay, a two-mile stretch of fine-white sand that arcs towards Benbane Head. From the hills above the beach, you can hear the soft, steady sound of the distant waves and feel your heartbeat slow down to match their rhythms. I cycled through a narrow, hedge-lined backroad that meanders down to the Giant's Causeway, where columns of layered hexagonal rocks recede into the sea and eventually reappear at Fingal's Cave in the Scottish island of Iona. Families were sitting on the stones, eating picnics and taking pictures, enjoying a day of tranquillity on a coastline that had been forged by violent volcanic activity millions of years beyond comprehension. The crust of the Earth suddenly appeared very thin, and even the certainties of solid ground started to seem suspect.

On the Sunday, I decided to hike the Causeway coast back towards Ballintoy, the most spectacular and spellbinding walk in all of Ireland. This is the land of Fionn mac Cumhaill, the land of surreal shapes and spirits. The cliffs before Benbane Head turned themselves into the pipes of a church organ, the huge rock on the shore became the discarded boot of a giant, the face of an ogre gazed out to sea from above the caves. I walked beside sea-stacks, inside cave-tunnels, under rock-arches, through a constantly shifting seascape, to the shelter of Portbradden and its tiny church that clings to the shoreline. I continued across the beach of White Park Bay, where the sea that seems so inviting would suck you into its bitter-cold currents and send you to oblivion like the wooden boat of a child. And, finally, I reached the harbour of Ballintoy and rested in the small café where they serve you tea and scones, and ease you back to the familiar world.

The coast road carries on from the Causeway to the town of Portstewart and the banks of the Bann. I cycled past the ruins of Dunseverick Castle, where the rulers of the Northern World once lived, and where the southern road took you directly to the High Kings of Tara. Now, there are only fragments of a famous past, and a narrow path that leads to a neglected harbour. A few miles further on, Dunluce Castle stands above the sea, its Norman towers imposing themselves on earlier and weaker fortifications. For over four hundred years, it was the most powerful fortress in Ulster, designed to last forever. But in the end, it too began to crumble into the cliffs, unable to withstand the sea-changes of centuries.

And so to Portstewart, with its cliff paths and sand-dunes, and its strand that stretches towards the sunset. I walk along the beach in the quiet of the evening, before the day dissolves in darkness. And as I walk, I begin to hear the soft sound of tennis balls on distant cricket bats. My father is bowling underarm spinners at the makeshift wicket behind me; I am trying to hit the ball beyond his reach, into the boundary of the sand-dunes. There are families and towels and bathing suits and kids, there are square-back cars with crank-shaft handles, there are jellyfish stranded on the shore. I run with my friends into the sea and jump over the waves to keep warm, splashing with my arms and legs. I take my bucket and spade, and dig channels and rivers, and build towering castles in the sand. I go back to our towel on the beach and challenge my father to a game of hide-and-seek in the dunes. I run and run and run, dodging and weaving through the hills, determined that he will not find me. I dart further and further into the dunes, keeping low, hiding in hollows, hugging the hillsides, crossing a river, completely alone, completely lost. Climb to the highest sand-dune, try to find the sea, try to find the beach, try to find the towel, try to find my father. Trapped on the far side of the river, tired, scared, scrambling across sand-spits, following footsteps of strangers, finding square-back cars, crawling like a jellyfish, falling into my father's arms, falling down, falling asleep, falling, falling.

I walk along the beach in the quiet of the evening, before the day dissolves in darkness. And as I walk, I hear the waves rolling onto the shore and see the sand-dunes dimming in the twilight. Ahead, in the distance, there is an old man walking his dog by the water's edge. He is throwing a stick into the sea; the dog runs through the waves, retrieves the stick, shakes himself dry. The man bends down slowly, picks up the stick, throws it again. The sun is setting over North Atlantic waters, diffusing faded light through sea and sky, glowing like the embers of a dying fire, before it too vanishes from view.

The Hills of Donegal

"It seems there are two arts which some god gave to mankind, music and gymnastics," said Socrates in the dark days before there were bicycles, "not for the soul and body incidentally, but for the harmonious adjustment of the two." Music runs through your mind when you're cycling, following the pace of the pedals, matching the mood of the day, sometimes lively, sometimes wistful, making its own harmonies. Riding along the remote back roads of eastern Donegal, past fields of sheep and cows and horses, the tunes are easy and slow – "'Tis Pretty to Be in Ballinderry," "Carolan's Draught," "Danny Boy." "Danny Boy" came to me as I cycled through Limavady earlier in the day, the town where Jane Ross learnt the tune from an itinerant fiddler back in 1851. And although it's been sentimentalized, elevatorized, even Elvisized, the melody is simply too beautiful and too haunting to stay on the shelves of Irish schlock.

There was a time, though, when I swore I would never play the tune again. It was in southern Ontario, when I was with a band called the Nearly Famous Folk Group, singing songs from the sixties and desperately hoping that a folk revival would sweep us to success. We had just finished a set consisting mainly of recycled Joan Baez and Leonard Cohen songs, when a very drunk man in a suit staggered from his barstool to the stage and slurred out a semi-coherent request for "Danny Boy." We looked at each other, uncertainly; this did not fall within our usual repertoire of Deep and Meaningful Songs, in which the depth usually obscured the meaning. But, after a brief consultation, we decided to give it a try. Marie, our singer, had a classically trained voice and put it to full operatic effect; she filled the room with her singing and stunned the bar into silence – something we'd never achieved before, not even with our version of "Hava Nagila."

When we had finished, the man with the suit lurched towards us and swayed like a ship's mast in a storm. "That was the best version of …" he began, his words fading away into an alcoholic vapour trail. He tried again. "That was the best version of 'Danny Boy' I've ever –" The next word should probably have been "heard." But it actually came out as a long "urrrrr," and then "urrrrrach," followed immediately with the complete contents of a huge and heaving stomach – beer, to be sure, together with half-digested hamburger, bits of yellow stuff, and various types of unidentifiable animal remains. It travelled in slow motion towards the stage, and then splattered the singer of "Danny Boy," sticking like warm glue to her skirt, her stockings, her shoes.

Marie looked at me, with eyes of shock, eyes of anger. "Never again," she said. "Never again," I agreed.

But that was long ago and far away, and the tune is going through my head on a summer's day on a remote road in eastern Donegal. I sat by the side of a field, took out the whistle, and let the melody ride on the breeze, past wild purple orchids and rhododendrons, across farmland and flowers.

> But come ye back, when summer's in the meadow
> Or when the valley's hushed and white with snow
> 'Tis I'll be there, in sunshine or in shadow
> Oh Danny Boy, oh Danny Boy, I love you so.

The sheep kept chewing on the grass; the cows lay still in the fields, blinking the flies away. A stray car passed by, the driver lazily raising his index finger from the steering wheel in the familiar Donegal acknowledgment of strangers.

The road is rough here. It rattles your bones, sending sharp currents of electricity shooting through your fingers and forearms. It vibrates through the saddle and creates a condition that all male cyclists experience, but few talk about – the much-feared Penile

Numbness Syndrome. It's a weird feeling, or lack of feeling; you gradually realize that all sensation has stopped in the place where your penis used to be. The immediate psychological effect is somewhat unsettling. You try squeezing your groin muscles together to find signs of life, but nothing happens. At this point, your fears tend to increase; the only thing that's rising is your sense of panic. You want to reach down inside your pants to check that everything really is where it's supposed to be and to nurture it back to life. But such a strategy can be liable to misinterpretation, especially in areas of high population density. So there's only one thing for it: you must get off your bicycle, find the nearest toilet, get in the cubicle, and clutch yourself tightly until everything returns to normal. If nothing happens after twenty minutes, don't bother calling the doctor; it's too late.

If this condition occurs in the Republic, where the quality of the roads is directly linked to the power of the local politicians, there is one thing you should know as you rush to the toilet. You might think that the word MNÁ on the door is the work of a dyslexic sign painter and that you are heading safely into the men's room. If so, you would be mistaken. And the consequences of your mistake could be rather unfortunate, especially if you're hoping to leave the country with a clean criminal record. In fact, MNÁ is Irish for women, and FIR is the word for men. At least, that's what they tell me.

The next day, I moved from the hills of Donegal to the Glenveagh Mountains, where saw-toothed ridges cut into the sky and green fields merge into rust-brown uplands. Travelling through the moors, you can see the flat-topped Muckish Mountain ahead, a pig's back stretched out against the horizon. A bend in the road suddenly brings Errigal Mountain into view, like a giant cockleshell turned on its side. There is a strong wind at my back, sweeping across the grass; the road runs by mountain streams fed by mountain lakes. This is a vast, howling, elemental landscape, which seems to go on forever; there's a turf-cutter in the distance and no one else for miles. It is now twelve o'clock; back in Toronto, it's seven in the morning. The cars are beginning to crowd together on the 401, packing the Don Valley Parkway bumper to bumper, filling the city with a clinging cloud of exhaust fumes, crawling towards a lake where fish cannot live and people cannot swim. But here, the air is pure and the streams are clear; here, there is only the sky, the mountains, and the soft purples and greens of the moorlands.

Driven by the wind, I pass beside the scree-scraped slopes of Errigal, above the long lake that reaches towards Gweedore and the Donegal coast, where Irish is still spoken as a first language. Narrow roads take you from Bunbeg, through the Rosses, to Burtonport and Dungloe, towns that are feeding on tourism. Country-and-western music is everywhere, piped through speaker systems, played on the radio, coming out of pub windows. It's far and away the most popular form of music in Ireland, with disco as a close second; traditional music is much further down on the list, even here in the heart of the *Gaeltacht*, the Irish-speaking area. Sometimes you encounter bizarre musical mutations – country-and-western songs in the Irish language, country-and-Gaelic if you like, complete with all the subtleties of the genre, such as key changes. Most of the music, though, is in English; you get the latest hits from Nashville, alongside home-grown Irish songs performed by home-grown heroes like Big Tom.

The American connection isn't really as surprising as it seems; some of the classic country and cowboy songs simply grafted American words onto Irish tunes. "The Streets of Laredo" originated as a song about the Irish patriot Robert Emmet, and, from the other side of the political divide, "The Old Orange Flute" provided the melody for "Sweet Betsy from Pike." More recently, Bob Dylan extended the process into the world of folk music; songs like "Restless Farewell" and "I Pity the Poor Immigrant" are reworkings of Irish ballads. There are other similarities; in both the Irish singing tradition and American bluegrass music, the emotional range encompasses no more than two degrees, whether the subject of the song is a train wreck, finding Jesus, or strolling down the road and having a smoke. In many ways, the west of Ireland is closer to the United States than it is to Britain; the next parish, as they say in Donegal, is New York.

Still, there are differences as well. American country songs are mainly about hurtin', lyin' and cheatin', with layer upon layer of Pain and Self-Pity, like a wedding cake when the cream has gone sour. In one verse alone your dog can be run over by a pick-up truck and your mother can be called home to heaven, while your chick-babe leaves you for another man, the finance company repossesses your home, and your last whiskey bottle is drained of everything but your own tears. Generally speaking, the songs fall neatly into three categories: Before Divorce, Divorce, and After Divorce. But they don't allow divorces in Ireland, on the assumption that comely lads and lasses live happily ever after, or at least that "till death do us part" really means what it says, for better or for worse. Country-and-Irish music is thick with the syrup of sentimentality, with countless variations on the "we still love each other after all these years" theme. There's also a strong streak of nostalgia, of the kind that can romanticize "Dublin in the rare ould times" while conveniently forgetting that the city used to have the highest death rate in the Western world.

In Bunbeg, Burtonport, and Dungloe, I inquire at local pubs about traditional music sessions, and am told that "it's too early in the season," that "there's not enough demand for it around here," that "the musicians charge too much money nowadays." It's seen as a commodity for tourist consumption, rather than something that people play for its own sake, for their own enjoyment.

The demands of tourism contradict the spirit of sessions. Tourism requires order and regularity – times posted on a pub window: "Traditional Music Tonight, Starts 9.30" – so that people know where and when things are happening. But sessions are by their very nature unpredictable and spontaneous; they seem to spring up out of nothing. When traditional musicians get together for a session, the last thing they think about is the time of the year, or the state of popular demand – although a few free pints would go down well enough. They are there to share a few tunes, a few laughs, and a few drinks; they are there, in short, for the fun of it. And if other people share the enjoyment, well, so much the better.

There's no doubt that tourism has helped the west; it brings in the money, provides hard-up musicians with something approaching an income, and breathes new life into the area each summer. But, in line with the Heisenberg Principle, the act of observing changes the character of that which is being observed. Once a session is performed for an audience, it is no longer a session. You wind up with a commercial version of a communal activity, and you separate the music from the culture that sustained it in the first place. It's part of a wider problem: tourists are attracted to the area largely because of its hospitality, its slower pace of life, its distinct culture; but tourism is subtly altering the culture by turning it into a marketable commodity, by making it self-conscious. At its best, tourism promises to reinvigorate the region, to give it new energy and life. At its worst, it threatens to turn the west of Ireland into the largest Theme Park in Europe.

Leaving Dungloe on a bright, breezy morning, I cycled by bogland and mountain, past the beautiful Gweebarra Bay where the sandbars almost touch each other. At a village shop near Glenties, I met up with an old fellow whose molecules were mixed into an equally old bicycle; he was dressed in a faded brown suit and looked as if he'd stepped out of a sepia photograph. He inspected my bike carefully and closely, with its wide tires and its multiplicity of gears, and marvelled at the technology. I inspected his bike equally closely, with its heavy black frame and its complete absence of gears, and marvelled at his stamina. "You'd need to be in pretty good shape to handle these hills on that bike," I said. "Well now," he replied, "I'm getting on a bit, you know, so I have to walk up a few of them." And off he went, bolt upright on the saddle, cycling steadily up a hill that would break your back, waving goodbye without turning around, and probably smiling to himself as well.

At Ardara, I wandered into Peter Oliver's pub, where the walls were lined with pictures of fiddle and accordion players, a photographic history of traditional music in Donegal. Beside the pictures there were ancient, played-out instruments, leaning on the wall like old bicycles. The session scene was stronger in those days, Peter said, the days when the fiddle and accordion players had packed the pub with music, and the instruments on the wall had been full of life. "All the older players are dying off," he said, "and the younger ones are emigrating."

Still, I wonder if he is right; young people have been leaving the west for generations now, but the tradition lives on. In Ardara, Peter and his daughter kept it going themselves and started a session of their own later in the evening. He played the accordion, guitar, and mandolin (not at the same time, though; he was talented, but not that talented), and his daughter played a sweet-sounding fiddle, while the barman poured some of the smoothest Guinness in the world. It may not have been as lively or as brilliant as the sessions of old, but it was good enough; the fellows looking out from the photographs would have waved and maybe smiled as well.

The next morning began slowly; I sat outside on a park bench, recovering from the revelry, steeling myself for the ride up the Glengesh Pass to Glencolumbkille. It was one of those rare, clear, cloudless days that sharpens the senses and brings everything into focus. Just south of Ardara, I turned west along the mountain road towards Glengesh, tracing the course of a rapid-flowing river that coiled its way back to the coast, past sheep's wool fleeced on barbed-wire fences, the hares running through the fields, and the butterflies dancing lightly over wild flowers. A gentle, rolling slip-jig called "The Butterfly" floats into mind; it could have been composed on a day like this, in a place like this, so well does it fit the feeling. And then, gradually at first, the road begins to steepen, and turns into a heart-pounding haul of increasingly impossible spirals, drawing all the energy out of you, until it finally flattens out. I stop, rest, and play the whistle to the valley below, to the winding road turning in tune with the stream, and to the distant Blue Stack mountains in the east, at one with the music, at peace with the rhythms of the day.

A few miles later, Glencolumbkille comes into view, below the mountains and before the sea, the place where Saint Columbkille once travelled as he sought to graft Christianity onto the culture of the Celts. There are ancient, mysterious pagan monuments here, standing upright like Christianized phalluses beside the Anglican church. And beyond them lies Glen Bay, sheltered by high cliffs splintering into the sea, where the sunset suffuses the sky with a soft-red haze and the waves pulse in like the heartbeat of another world. I walk back to the village, under constellations of stars, points of light from pre-Christian times, and hear drifts of music coming out of distant windows. But this time I do not go in; I want this space, this openness, this place where past meets present, land meets sea, earth meets sky, in the vast silence of the night.

And then, sometime in the darkness, the silence shuddered with the wind, clouds closed in from the north, and the sound of rain began to rap on sleeping houses. It angled in on the streets, black and cold, drenching early risers, driving people back into doorways. As the morning went on, the wind became stronger and the angle became sharper – unrelenting, unremitting rain, looking like it would fall forever. Cycle through Ireland for any length of time and it will eventually catch up with you. Liquid sunshine, they call it, coming down in buckets from the sky. Local weather forecasters will share their wisdom with you: "If you can see Aran Island, it's going to rain," a Donegal man told me in Burtonport; "if you can't see it, it's already raining." "It only rained twice last summer," someone else said; "the first time from May to June, and second time from July to August."

What to do? I'd like to wait until it passes, but then I could be caught in Glencolumbkille for the rest of my life. So, I resigned myself to getting soaked, and set off reluctantly up the ferocious hill that takes you out of town towards Carrick and Kilcar. I try to be philosophical about the situation: You need the rain to appreciate the sun; you need the hills to appreciate the plains; you need

the wind against you to appreciate the wind behind you. But I don't mean a word of it. All I want is a dry day, a road that always runs downhill, and a breeze that is permanently at my back.

Away to my left, high on Glen Head, the distant ruin of a grey tower looks out over a grey sea; it is eventually enveloped by black Atlantic clouds and blotted out by the rain. Like the sea mirroring the sky, the moorland changes colours with the weather and becomes as dark and green and heavy as a sponge, while the mountains appear and disappear through a thick wet mist. A few miles out of Glencolumbkille, I turned off the road towards blustery Bunglass, up the steep and narrow track to Slieve League, where cloud-shrouded cliffs sheer down two thousand feet to the sea. A bitter north wind sweeps showers of rain across the hills, saturating everything in its path. A soft day, as they say; a soft day with a fresh breeze; I wouldn't like to experience a hard one.

By the time I reached Killybegs, I was ready for a drink. The pub was full of fishermen, who'd just come back from ten days of hauling cod and whitefish out at Rockall; it was only lunchtime, and they were already three sheets to the wind. "I hate fishing," said one of them. "I'm a trained carpenter, not a bloody fisherman. Is there any work for carpenters in Canada?" Tommy, his mate, hated fishing as well; he was heading out that night on the Galway bus, looking for some other kind of work, any other kind of work, anywhere but here. He put his arm around me, eyes half-closed from alcohol, and smiled blearily: "You're a bollix." And then, for emphasis: "You're a right fuckin' bollix." I'm not entirely sure, but I'd like to think that this was a friendly greeting; generally speaking, it's when people stop insulting you that you have to start worrying. Holding me in a half-embrace, he began to sing "Fiddler's Green," a song about the final resting place of fishermen:

> Now, Fiddler's Green is a place I've heard tell
> Where fishermen go if they don't go to hell
> Where the weather is fair and the dolphins do play
> And the cold coasts of Greenland are far far away.

And then the chorus:

> Wrap me up in my oilskins and jumper
> No more to the docks I'll repair
> Just tell my old shipmates I'm taking a trip mates
> And I'll see you one day in Fiddler's Green.

I try to join in, but have trouble following him through a maze of modulations; he changed key more times than a country-and-western singer on speed. "You're a right fuckin' bollix of a bollix," he said. I began to worry that I would be trapped there for the rest of the day, held in a permanent arm-lock, singing off-key, swopping prolix bollix stories until the Galway bus carried him away. There was only one thing for it – the old Escape through the Men's Toilet trick. Out the side-door, into the yellowing yard where rain and urine and beer swilled together in the gutter, over the wall, down the alley, and back on the bicycle. Hou-fuckin'-dini would have been proud.

I cycled on to Mountcharles and Donegal Town, before turning southwards to Ballyshannon, home of one of Ireland's finest folk festivals. After checking into a bed-and-breakfast on the Bundoran road, proprietor Mary Doherty, I walked back to the town centre and took in the scene. There was a marquee at the bottom of the hill, holding the formal concerts, where the folkies happily listened to the music in a kind of self-created cigarette-free zone. And there were pubs all around, holding the informal sessions, where everyone else in town laughed and drank and happily choked themselves to death on nicotine. A Canadian friend once suggested to me that someone should organize package Smokers' Tours to Ireland, as one of the last places in the Western world where you can inhale with impunity – Guilt-Free Smoking in the *Gaeltacht*, Nicotine Nirvana Holidays Incorporated, Toxic Tours of Tipperary.

I started with the clear air of the concerts and the brilliant music of groups like Donegal's own Altan, with their dazzling array of fast-paced jigs and reels. Some people complain that they are too fast, and that the music gets lost in the rush. But their playing explodes with energy, and they combine speed with subtlety; it's the kind of thing you could listen to all day and all night. There were singer-songwriters as well, people like Kieran Goss with his mischievous smile and deadpan humour, singing Tom Paxton's folk classic "The Last Thing on my Mind," and adding an extra verse for good measure:

> Well I met this young lass at a folk club
> Like you do, like you do.
> So I bought her a drink and we chatted
> Wouldn't you, wouldn't you.
> And then after the show, she invited me home
> Said our interests were one of a kind.
> Then she played me every record that Tom Paxton ever made
> And you know that was the Last Thing on my Mind.

Dolores Keane and John Faulkner were up next, two of the finest traditional singers around, giving us songs like "The Bonny Light Horseman," about a woman lamenting the death of her lover in the Napoleonic Wars, and "Sliabh Gallion Braes," about emigration from Ireland – death and emigration being compulsory themes in all traditional song sets. Dolores was mildly inebriated, and so were we; the chorus of "Sliabh Gallion Braes" was loud enough to lift the marquee off its moorings.

And then we came down with a bump. The last singer of the night was so bad that I have blocked his name from memory; he was a very large man with a very loud voice, a veteran from the

and exhilarated, I walked slowly back along the road
and the bed-and-breakfast. As I opened the door, Mrs
eared out of nowhere, wearing her dressing gown,
patula. "Have you eaten tonight?" she inquired as I
; yes I have thanks," I replied, lying through my teeth.
ed as green as a plate of fried tomatoes; I made up my
on my way first thing in the morning.

folk boom of the early sixties. When he sang raucous, rambunctious
drinking songs, full of the obligatory whack-fol-de-daddio's and
too-ra-loo-ra-loo's, he was just about listenable, if you liked that
sort of thing. It was when he attempted anything remotely requiring the least shred of sensitivity that he went beyond the boundaries
of the bearable. He took the most beautiful songs in the world and
pounded them into the ground; the effect was like a pneumatic drill
splitting through granite, or dental work without the anaesthetic.
After ten minutes, I ran for cover, only to find that there was no
escape. "I wish I was in Carrickfergus," he growled. So did I. But
his voice was so loud that you could probably hear him there as
well. It carried southwards to the moors of Cornwall, northwards
to the shores of Scotland, and eastwards to the Accursed Ridge of
Leinster. It pierced the hearts of all the people and terrified them,
so that men lost their colour and strength, women suffered miscar-
riages, children lost their senses, and animals and trees and soil and
water all became barren. "I heard him play at the Oxford Folk
Festival last May Eve," whispered a Welshman next to me, as if
afraid of being overheard; "if you want my opinion, he should be
locked in a stone chest and buried in the deepest fuckin' pit you
can find."

By the time he had stopped singing, I was back at the bed-and-
breakfast, dazed and disoriented, tired and emotional, cold and
hungry. Mrs Doherty, proprietor, was nothing if not flexible; knowing that sessions and concerts tend to run late, she offered a twenty-
four-hour breakfast service to cover all eventualities, from German
tourists who insisted on getting up at the ungodly hour of six in
the morning, to mad Irish musicians who were straggling in as the
Germans were checking out. "Have you eaten tonight?" she inquired
as I came in, still trying to scrape the gravel out of my ears. I shook
my head; she ordered me to sit down. And fifteen minutes later, a
classic Irish breakfast, the Ulster Fry, suddenly appeared on my plate
– fried eggs, fried sausages, fried tomatoes, fried bacon, fried soda
farls, fried potato bread, fried potatoes, fried white pudding and
fried black pudding, a veritable festival of cholesterol.

I was light-headed from drink and ready to eat a year's supply
of food. "Mmmm, this black thing tastes good," I said, slicing off

another sticky piece of pudding with my fork. "What is it?" "There are some questions that are best left unasked," she replied, smiling to herself and shovelling another round of hot, well-greased sausages onto my plate. But I knew what it was – black pudding, a euphemistic expression for congealed animal blood served up in layers of lard. In the cold light of sobriety, I wouldn't go within thirty-three miles of the stuff.

That night, I had strange dreams; I was running naked in a field of lettuces, feasting on salads, rolling in alfalfa sprouts and water cress. When I awoke, a thick sediment of sludge lay heavily on my stomach. I heaved myself into the shower and imagined that I could still smell the stuff frying in the pan. Slowly, horribly, it dawned on me that the aroma was all too real; down in the breakfast room, Mrs Doherty was serving up more of the same to unsuspecting guests. And, in true Donegal fashion, she was singing country-and-western songs while she was doing it: "My tears have washed I love you from the blackboard of my heart," "I'm Riding High in the Saddle Again," "Home, Home on the Range." She brought me a plate of Fried Everything, topped off with three extra black puddings. "Since you liked them so much last night," she said happily, "I thought I'd treat you to some more this morning."

Out on the streets, Ballyshannon was blinking back into life. Half-way up the hill, the Old Rope String Band began an open-air show of slapstick session music. They would start their pieces with slightly excessive seriousness, and then break into cheerfully controlled chaos – juggling the instruments with one other, performing acrobatic routines, making human pyramids, and never so much as missing a beat. In one song, "Fire, Fire, Fire," the fiddle player not only imitated the sound of a passing fire engine, but also threw in the doppler effect for good measure. At the time, he was balancing one leg on the head of the guitarist, who was himself standing on the shoulders on the banjo player. "Now that," said the man next to me, "that is a rare and a wonderful talent."

Down the road, on the rooftop terrace at Sweeny's pub, a bagpiper was tearing through "The Atholl Highlanders," one of the most energetic jigs ever written; pints of lager were accumulating around him in appreciation. At the Thatch pub on top of the hill,

three sessions were going
and accordionists straddle
a stupor. Upstairs, in the
table and exchanged song
the main room, bunged w
erent, outrageous Silly Soι
done-to-death Irish songs
Rover," or Ice-T attacking '

At one point, an Americ
everyone to be serious for a
earnestness: "I'd feel very pr
to sing a song which meant
up in Chicago, and which sti
It's a song about an island w
– an island beset by conflict,
its sense of humour; an islan
on it, but an island that cann
compelled to leave. Please rais
he launched straight into the

By late afternoon, the sessi
Outside the Thatch, I played
dancers who wove around ea
tapestry. Then it was down the
trail of old chip-bags to the m
night of Celtic-jazz-rock music
best uilleann pipers, and his b
Celtic music and jazz are botl
around set themes, and deep in
there's a rock n' roll star trying
the uilleann pipes and the saxop
then wheeled and dipped and sc
lead guitarist drilled out deep-p
drums split the sky. There was a v
drove us to our feet and carried u
were silhouetted against the sta
strings of sound, shaken into life l
us like an Atlantic storm blowing

Exhausted
to Bundoran
Doherty apɩ
wielding a s
came in. "Ye
My face turr
mind to be

The Tar Road
to Sligo

Ireland is the only country in the world where you can experience all four seasons in one day. I left Ballyshannon in a soft rain, cycling by the flowers of spring; by the time I reached Bundoran, it was the first month in summer, a day of sunny banks and green meadows. But later in the afternoon, dark clouds began to gather over autumn woods; and when I rounded Benbulben mountain on the tar road to Sligo, it was the twenty-eighth of January and the hailstones were bouncing off my helmet.

Sligo is the home of Ireland's most precious poet, the remote, the spiritual, the ideal William Butler Yeats; the land of the gaels and the land of the gales. Coldness was cast on me as I passed by the Yeats Grave, just before the Yeats Tavern (Food Served Daily) where the tour buses were pulling in. A few miles down the road, you could arise and go to Inishfree Motor Factors Company Ltd, and drive your car with peace of mind. Fingers were fumbling in the greasy till. Romantic Ireland was dead and gone; commercial Ireland was making a killing.

If you want to understand a people properly, someone once said, you should take their dominant self-image and turn it upside down. Canadians think of themselves as a northern people and identify with the wilderness; the vast majority of them actually live as far south as they can get and enjoy the most centrally heated civilization on Earth. The English think of themselves as a garden people and identify with images of rustic beauty; in fact, they are crowded into cities and live in one of the most industrialized countries in the world. The Irish think of themselves as a nation of romantics and identify with their Great Writers; but cycling through Sligo, you get the sense that they are really one of the most practical people on the planet, ready and willing to milk their cultural heritage for all it's worth, and maybe a bit more besides.

The wind seared across the mountains, sweeping the storms in from the sea; you'd have a hard time finding anything romantic about this weather, at any rate. Somewhere near Drumcliff, I passed a farmgate with a forbidding sign: BEWARE OF BULL. There wasn't a bull or a cow or a pig or a sheep within nine miles. BEWARE OF BULL – the sign should be posted at every airport and seaport in the country, as a Government Health Warning to all unsuspecting visitors, alerting them to the perils awaiting an Innocent in Ireland. "There are two rules for survival here," a Canadian friend told me the day after she'd landed in the country. "First, don't believe anything that anyone tells you. And second, don't take anything or anyone seriously." She knew what she was talking about. The sense of humour consists not so much in the telling of jokes as in the making of stories; the laughter lies not in the punchline, but in the process. And the essential equipment is a very, very long piece of string.

It happened to me shortly after I arrived in Whitehead, when two characters whom I shall call Bernie and Harry (since those are their real names) took me for a ride in the country. We passed a field in the distance where there were buses, cars, flags, and streamers. "What's going on there?" I asked. Mistake number one: you think you are asking a simple question, but you are really setting yourself up. Bernie and Harry turned it into a kind of play:

Harry: Well now, I wouldn't like to say … I'm not sure, really … I wouldn't know.
Bernie: Best say nothing. (To me): Best forget that you ever saw anything. Fine day, now, isn't it?
Dupe: No, no, tell me. What's happening?
[Long silence]
Harry: Well, all right then. It's a Dog Worry, if you must know.
Dupe: What on Earth is a Dog Worry?
Bernie: (Incredulously) You don't know what a Dog Worry is? D'ye hear that, Harry; this fellow doesn't know what a Dog Worry is?

Harry:	Hmmmmph. Calls himself a student of Irish history, and he's never heard of a Dog Worry. What's the world coming to? Talk about declining standards of education.
Bernie:	Well, now. Have you ever heard of a cock fight?
Dupe:	(Nods).
Harry:	Well that's something, I suppose. At least he's heard of a cock fight; there's hope for the world yet.
Bernie:	A Dog Worry is just like a cock fight, except they use dogs. They dig a large pit, and throw in a couple of dogs. After the animals have a good set-to, they pull out the winner and bury the loser.
Harry:	Alsations, usually, although pit-bulls are becoming more popular these days.
Bernie:	It's an old Irish custom. I'm very surprised you've not heard of it.

Now, I'm an unreconstructed dog lover – as they very well knew – and although I have sometimes been theoretically seduced by notions of cultural relativism, I find that I don't hold with them at all when I actually meet them in practice. "I don't care whether it's an old Irish custom or not," I said; "it's disgusting and it ought to be stopped." Time to slacken the line a little; the more string, the more fun.

| Harry: | Ah, well, I'm not saying it's good and I'm not saying it's bad, but still it is illegal nowadays, you know. |

Bernie: It is, it is. But that doesn't stop people from doing it all the same. Just look at all the coaches and cars out there.

Harry: True enough. It's even rumoured that you'll find the occasional priest going along as well. Sure it's part of our heritage, whatever way you look at it.

Dupe: (With excessive moral indignation) Taking two dogs, throwing them in a pit, making them tear each other to pieces, and burying the loser – that's absolutely barbaric.

Bernie: Not at all, not at all. In a barbaric country they would bury the winner as well.

They never did tell me what was actually happening; it was only the next day I learned from a friend that I had really witnessed the crowds gathering for a Gaelic football game. I would like to think that he was telling the truth.

BEWARE OF BULL – on the streets, in a car, in a pub (especially in a pub), in a restaurant, in a house; take nothing on trust, and assume that you are surrounded by congenital liars. I once heard a story about a woman who invited two people who did not know each other for dinner. Beforehand, she told the first guest that the other was a bit deaf, so he'd have to speak loudly and distinctly; then she told the other that the first was a bit odd. And with that, she sat down to enjoy the meal. BEWARE OF BULL – anywhere, everywhere, except in an empty field just outside Drumcliff.

And so to Sligo, to dry out and rest before a weekend of music. I walked along the riverbank and watched the swans resting on the water. Suddenly, there was a sharp sound like wire whipping through the air; turning around, I saw a swan in full flight, with its straight, outstretched neck and its powerful wings, heading for home. Further up the river, I came to the Blue Lagoon Discotheque, where Sharon Shannon and her band would be giving a concert later in the evening. Sharon Shannon has two things going for her: she is an excellent accordionist and she has the nicest smile in Ireland. The combination is unbeatable.

In the bar, before the show, she was sitting with her band around the TV set, watching the opening ceremonies of the Eurovision

Song Contest. One of the best things about living in North America is that you don't get this thing inflicted on you every year – a succession of Ever-So-Nice singers from every country in Europe, singing a succession of Instantly Forgettable songs, followed by a succession of Politically Dubious votes to decide the winner. The definition of Europe is expansive enough to include countries as far apart as Iceland and Israel; this makes for a rather long evening. And because a successful song must appeal to all cultures and all languages, the principle of the Lowest Common Denominator kicks in with mathematical certainty. You want to write a song that will appeal equally to people who speak Turkish, Hungarian, and Danish? Cut down on words from your own language – after all, these are necessarily exclusive – and replace them with lively banging noises that everyone can enjoy and understand. Fill your song with lots of bings and bongs and billy-billy bongs, make sure that your singer smiles a lot, and pray that the English judges haven't got it in for you. The total effect can only be described as mind-numbing; you'd be better off trapped in an elevator with the Singing Nun. Ireland has been winning the Eurovision Song Contest a lot recently, almost as a matter of routine – a trend that I, for one, find distinctly disturbing.

But the music in the Blue Lagoon was much more exciting, vibrant, and creative than anything coming out of the contest; there was nothing remotely bland, boring, or banal about the Sharon Shannon band. She sat on a chair in the middle of the stage, moving from light-hearted waltzes to high-speed reels, deep inside her own world, thoroughly immersed in the music, swaying and smiling with the currents that flow beneath it all. Accordion, fiddle, guitar, and bass were rushing and running together, thundering into a breakneck finish with "The Foxhunter's Reel," leaving us shouting and stamping for more. Meanwhile, in the other room, Ireland was busy winning yet another Eurovision Song Contest.

There is never any shortage of traditional music in Sligo. The next day, I made my way down to TD's pub for the regular Sunday afternoon After-Mass Session. At first, I thought I was in the wrong place. The sound system was playing the kind of country-and-Irish music that would make you cringe – "That's the Way the Girls Are from Texas," sung in a fake American accent that actually outstripped the fake Irish accents you hear in America: Sligo's Revenge for those old Bing Crosbie movies, with all their begorrah's and top o'the mornin's.

But then the sound system was shut off, and three fellows started up on piano and fiddle and accordion. Before you knew it, the man at the next table moved to the centre of the floor and began a dazzling display of dancing, arms straight, legs flying, feet beating out syncopated rhythms to the reels. And when he'd finished, another man from another table got up and tried to outdance him, amid shouts and cheers of encouragement. For the next half hour or so, just about every able-bodied male in the pub got up to dance, while I hid in the corner behind the Sunday paper, for safety's sake.

An uilleann piper, another accordionist, and a guitarist settled themselves around the musicians' table and took the session into high gear. "What's that tune called?" someone asked after a particularly lively set of reels. Now one thing you can be sure of about session musicians is that they never know the names of the tunes they're playing; it's almost a point of honour with them not to know. But that never stops them from making up answers on the spot, in much the same way that someone who hasn't a clue about the location of the pub you're trying to find won't shrink from giving you directions anyway. "That was 'The Sow's Lament over the Empty Trough,'" said the piper. "Not at all," replied the fiddler; "it was 'My Mother Drowned in the Holy Water at Lourdes.'" BEWARE OF BULL flashed in imaginary neon through my mind.

But it's true that the same tune can have a dozen different names, just as the same name can have a dozen different tunes. A jig like "The Black Rogue" has, appropriately enough, an assortment of aliases: "Come under My Plaiddie," "'Tis a Bit of a Thing," "The Irish Lass," "Nature and Melody," "Johnny McGill," "Michael Malloy," and "Tom Linton," to name but a few. And there are at least six different pieces that go under the name of "The Lark on the Strand." Some of the names are so bizarre that they're in no need of a little bull to help them along: "Johnny with the Queer Thing," "The Gudgeon of Maurice's Car," or "Wallop the Spot," not to mention "Cock Up Your Beaver," about which no questions should be asked.

Traditional music is nothing if not fluid; particular tunes will be popular for a while, fade into obscurity, and re-surface some time in the future. To survive in sessions, you have to be able to learn tunes quickly. You could tape a session, spend the following year learning all the pieces, and find when you returned that the musicians had moved on to a completely different repertoire; it's hard on beginners, but it keeps the music fresh.

On occasions, the music will flow back into itself and form cyclical patterns through the streams. A friend of mine once taped a reel from the fiddle playing of Paddy Glackin during a late-night kitchen hooley. He took the tape home, learnt the tune, and incorporated it into his repertoire. Not knowing its name, in the true traditional manner, he called it "Paddy Glackin's Reel." More than ten years later, he found himself playing once again in a session with the Man Himself; fortified with alcohol, he started into the reel, expecting Paddy to join in. But Paddy just sat there, listening closely, and nodding approvingly. "That's a fine tune," he said when it was over. "Where did you pick that one up?" And by way of thanks, my friend taught it back to Paddy.

After "The Sow's Lament over the Empty Trough," the session at TD's ran towards Holy Hour, when the pubs are supposed to close for an afternoon break. The musicians finished up in an unorthodox way; they broke into a kind of free-form Celtic-Chaos meltdown, full of clashing keys and discords, with each player trying to be more outrageous than the other. "That was called 'A Clatter of Shite,'" said the guitarist when it was over, giving birth to yet another new title. But it's hard to close a pub in the middle of the day, and things weren't quite over yet. An old fellow commandeered the fiddle and began to play The Greatest Hits of Vera Lynn – "We'll Meet Again," "The White Cliffs of Dover," you name it. He was in his element; there was no stopping him. Realizing this, and acting on the principle that if you can't beat them you might as well join them, the guitarist started to accompany him with beautiful, haunting jazz chords. When the fiddler had finally exhausted his repertoire of Vera Lynn tunes, he suddenly broke into a foot-stomping version of "The Irish Washerwoman," and then just as suddenly stopped. "There's nothing more I can do with it," he said, as he handed the fiddle back to its owner. He drained his glass, said goodbye, and wandered out the door.

The streets of Sligo were full of life; there were face painters and clowns and acrobats and magicians, drawing circles of people around them. Half-way up the hill, there was a marvellous man dressed in bright sunshine yellow, top hat over grey hair, sitting behind a bright red row of wooden dancing puppets. He played a cymbal with one foot, and with the other tapped on a board that set the puppets in motion; this was street entertainment straight from the nineteenth century, and it was still pulling in the crowds. It was as if he had stepped out of a song, a song about the Liverpool puppeteer Seth Davey, who had delighted thousands of kids outside Paddy's Market back in the 1890s:

> He sat on the corner of Bevington Bush,
> 'stride an old packing case,
> And the dolls on the end of the plank
>   went dancing,
> as he crooned with a smile on
>   his face:
> Come day, go day, wish in me
>   heart for Sunday,
> Drinking buttermilk all the
>   week, whiskey on a Sunday.

And from time to time, you could catch him taking a surreptitious swig from the mickey of whiskey that was concealed in his coat pocket.

In the evening, I made my way to McLynn's pub, tucked away on a side street, for one more Sligo session, before moving on to Mayo. Donal McLynn, the owner, was in the back room, playing the guitar with a couple of friends and singing a wide range of contemporary folksongs; soft voices filled the room for the chorus of "Caledonia," Dougie McLean's lovesong to Scotland, and for American tunes like "Boulder to Birmingham." Everyone was welcome to join in, or to take the lead for a while. An American with a hammer dulcimer played a delicate, lilting version of "The Butterfly" slipjig, bringing memories into this crowded room of the open spaces and soft air of the Glengesh Pass. And then, a well-dressed man who looked vaguely familiar, someone you might have seen on TV, was invited to sing. He was introduced as Joe Hunt, back in Sligo after making his seventh record, en route from Las Vegas to the Talk of the Town in Palma. He had a voice like a night-club singer, smooth as treacle, an Irish Willie Nelson. Like the other floor singers, he was given the regular two songs; in his case, "You Were Always on my Mind" and "For the Good Times." He certainly would not have looked or sounded out of place in Las Vegas or in Palma. But, as always, BEWARE OF BULL.

The Humours of Westport

I left Sligo on the Dublin road, before turning west towards the Ox Mountains of Mayo. Had I kept going southwards, I would have come to famous Ballymote and slightly less famous Knockgrania, birthplace of Michael Coleman, one of Ireland's greatest fiddle players. The land here is poor; the Coleman family, like many others, eked out a living as small farmers and turf-cutters. But the culture was rich; towards the end of the last century, when Michael was born, the local parish of Killavil was bursting at the seams with fiddle players – farmers, publicans, carpenters, blacksmiths, and quarrymen who lived for their music, and who transmitted the tradition to the next generation. There was dancing, too; Ireland was criss-crossed by dancing masters who would stay with local families, like the Colemans, and teach them the complex patterns of the steps.

Coming from a musical home – his father played the flute, and the house was a centre for ceilidhs – Michael soaked up the culture and soon won a reputation for his fiddling and dancing. The neighbours would take down the door when he visited and lay it on the floor, to give him a hard surface for tapping out the slipjigs. He was, as they said, very handy with his feet. But there were no jobs for him in Sligo, and, following a familiar pattern, he left for England in 1914 to find work as a labourer. When war broke out and there was talk of conscription, he decided to emigrate to America and wound up as a professional musician in New York, playing the fiddle in Irish clubs and pubs.

His arrival in New York coincided with the growth of the record industry, and in 1921 he signed his first contract with the Shannon label. They gave him something called a Stroh Violin, a fiddle with a metal horn attached to amplify the volume for recording purposes; it made the instrument sound harsh, and the musicians frequently felt like smashing it against the wall. But even now, when you listen to those old and scratchy recordings, the brilliance and vitality of his music come through. During the 1920s and 1930s, his records became immensely popular; they were sent back across the Atlantic to Ireland, where they influenced and inspired a whole generation of fiddle players.

For a while, Michael Coleman's music turned the Sligo style of playing into the dominant Irish style. His records became a standard against which other fiddlers would measure their own abilities, sometimes at the cost of their own distinctive regional styles. Still, local forms of playing have a way of reasserting themselves, and particular cultural traditions remain remarkably resilient in the face of modern homogenizing tendencies. As you travel through Ireland, you realize that fiddle playing in County Antrim, for example, is still sparser and plainer than that of County Sligo, say, or County Kerry. But in the end, a good fiddle player will learn in the way that Michael Coleman learnt – by listening to other people play, absorbing rather than imitating, mastering the basic techniques and then forgetting them, taking the music into the heart and letting it out again. And after that, regional traditions can take care of themselves.

It's ironic that Michael Coleman had to go to America to become famous in Ireland. The word in Knockgrania was that his older brother Jim was an even better player; but Jim stayed in Sligo, scratched out a living as a farmer, played for his friends, and let the notes die with him. No one today has ever heard of Jim Coleman. The United States was the magnet for traditional musicians; the Irish immigrants, with their communal networks and their strong memories of home, formed a natural and appreciative audience.

The best collection of traditional music was put together in America by Francis O'Neill, a flute player from Cork. He ran away from home in the 1880s, survived a shipwreck, and worked as a cowboy, schoolteacher, and railway clerk before joining the Chicago police force and winding up as its general superintendant. It may not be entirely coincidental that the Chicago police began to employ enough traditional Irish musicians to fill several ceilidh bands; there were rumours that the police fiddled while Chicago burned. But O'Neill used his skills as a detective to seek out tunes from the Irish immigrants who crowded into the city at the end of the last century, and the result was his *Music of Ireland*, published in 1903, which preserved well over a thousand pieces for posterity. It has become the Bible of Traditional Music; it's known simply as "the Book," and no self-respecting player would be seen dead without it.

With a strong northeasterly wind blowing behind me and the clouds threatening rain, I cycled with speed along the Ox Mountain road, through Coolaney and Clonacool and Mullany's Cross. The road is narrow and in places becomes little more than a track; there is no traffic to watch out for, and you feel free as you fly by the farms. Each village has an all-purpose shop and a pub; there aren't many tourists around here, and the people are hungry with hospitality. The day alternated between fast cycling and slow conversation, chatting leisurely with shopkeepers and publicans as if there was no tomorrow. Almost everyone I met had a relative in Canada; there seemed to be a minor exodus from the glens of Mayo to the suburbs of Mississauga, from these vast shadows to those vast shopping malls.

A few miles further on, I turned northwest towards Foxford and ran straight into a force fifteen gale. Black clouds rolled over the road; a hurricane of a headwind sent spears of ice-cold rain into my face. My jeans began to get thick and heavy with wetness; my shoes started to soak up the water. I pedalled for all I was worth to keep myself warm, but still couldn't stop my feet from freezing. Lorries and cars, indifferent to the blur of a bicycle on the road, were saturating me with their spray, cutting me close, disappearing into the distance.

And yet, in a perverse, masochistic way, I found it invigorating, exciting. "The Kesh Jig" raced through my mind, travelling with the turn of the pedals, driving me forward. Total concentration was required – fighting the storm, minding the cars, trying to keep warm, finding a home. I pushed past Lough Conn, dark as the sky, on the back road to Castlebar; suddenly, I was heading south again, with the wind behind me, and new strength in my legs. The landscape had an eerie, otherworldly quality, with heavy purples under a black haze of rain, in a wilderness of bogs, burnt-out brambles, gorse and grass; you could still catch the faint traces of charcoal in the rain, like an ashtray in water. It was as if some angry god had blasted the land; the place was haunted, dead roots twisting upwards from the ground like gnarled hands.

Bedraggled, besodden, and besmattered, I finally made it into Castlebar, looking like a drowned rat, and started knocking on bed-and-breakfast doors, until a kind-hearted landlady took me in and fed me tea and biscuits. I went upstairs, peeled off my clothes, and soaked myself in a hot bath – the hot bath of a lifetime, wrapping itself warmly around chilled bones, soothing away the tension from neck and shoulders, massaging the weariness from worn-out muscles. And then I slept for three days and three nights.

When my body had recovered, and the rain had eased into a gentle drizzle, I headed for Westport and the still snow-capped mountains of Mayo. I was travelling through Blessed Virgin Mary territory now; everywhere I went, statues of the BVM stood as silent surveyors of the moral landscape, imploring the traveller to find the Holy Spirit through the love of Mary. They remind me of dime-store plastic busts of Elvis, pale blue and white and tacky, religious icons turned to kitsch. The cult of Mary stretches back to eighth-century Ireland, but took its modern form in the early 1920s – extolling virginity, praising the spirit and damning the flesh, invoking rainstorms to put out the fires of sexual desire, crushing the head of the serpent. It's no wonder that Madonna's book on sex was banned in this land of Madonnas.

The cult of Elvis is the evening star to Mary's morning star. The serpent slid down his leg and turned into the Empire-State Erection, as he gyrated through his Greatest Hits and climaxed with wild pelvic thrusts – extolling hot-blooded physical passion, praising the flesh and damning the spirit, invoking fire-storms of lust, burning out of control. Elvis stands for sex without love; Mary stands for love without sex.

A few years ago, the statues began to send out signals of warning against the ways of sin. There were reports from Ballinspittle in south Cork that a couple of young girls, who spent their evenings gazing at statues, had seen the Blessed Virgin move. Others came and stared long and hard, until they saw it move as well. Before you knew it, crowds of thousands were flocking into Ballinspittle; the roads were widened, the village prospered, the bed-and-breakfasts flourished. And if it could happen in Ballinspittle, why not in the rest of the country? Everywhere you went, you would see knots of people gathered around BVMs, watching and waiting, waiting and watching, cars parked before statues.

Social commentators had a field day; they spoke of alienation, anxiety, nuclear war, and economic recession. The local bishop tried to distance himself from something that smacked too much of superstition. But still, the statues kept on moving; the apocalypse was in the air. There was a story afoot that a doctor had been driving on a remote country road, when he was confronted by a headless woman at a crossroads. She told him – precisely *how* she told him remains unclear – that the world was going to come to an end on the last day of September, when the wicked would finally be destroyed. But, through the goodness of God and the intercession of Mary, two countries would be spared from the general mayhem and wrath – Ireland and Poland. It wasn't clear whether Ireland included the North, where all those pesky Protestants lived. But if it did, Ian Paisley, the Free Presbyterians, and the Orange Order would owe a great deal more to the BVM than they would ever have cared to admit.

And so to Westport, where I meandered along the peaceful, wooded banks of the river, sat on the forest's edge, and rested with the whistle. Slow airs at first: "Down by the Salley Gardens," "Raglan Road," tunes with a wistful feel. And then some livelier pieces: "My Darling Asleep," "Apples in Winter," "The Milltown Jig."

Westport is well known for its music; with a little luck, there would be a good few jigs and reels later on that night.

Generally speaking, traditional music is not easy to find; nine times out of ten, you stumble across the sessions by accident. It's been that way for decades, even centuries. Back in 1802, Patrick Lynch came through Mayo on a song-collecting mission; by the time he reached Westport, he had worked out how it was done. "I am convinced," he wrote, "that the best way is to go to the shebeen-houses, and find out some little blasting schoolmaster, and warm his mouth with whiskey; and he will find out the singers for me." But in Westport today, you don't need to go knocking on doors or seeking out little blasting schoolmasters; for Westport is the home of Matt Molloy, the Roscommon flute player who performs with the Chieftains. Matt Molloy is to the flute what Michael Coleman was to the fiddle – a brilliant musician whose style has influenced an entire generation of players. And Matt Molloy has his own pub, right here in the centre of town.

I arrived early, determined to get as close to the musicians as possible. The session was in the back room, which was filling up with a wide variety of tourists – Austrians, Australians, Americans, French, the ubiquitous and inevitable Germans, everyone except the Irish. "We hear it all the time," said one regular who was staying in the front; "besides, it gets too crowded back there." And too crowded it was; we were squeezed together like a concertina, waiting for the music to start.

In the corner, some Americans were trying to explain the rules of baseball to an increasingly bewildered group of Australians; the Australians retaliated by trying to explain the rules of cricket to the Americans. It was hard to tell which side was winning. "How does the pitching work?" inquired the American. "It's called bowling, not pitching," said one of the Australians. "Well, it's like this. There are six balls in an over." "Unless there's a no-ball," chipped in his mate, helpfully, "in which case there are seven." "You mean the pitcher can have six balls before it's over?" the American asked, incredulously. "How many strikes does he have?" "Well, it's like this. He doesn't have any strikes unless he's batting, in which case he keeps on striking until he's out, or his partner's out, and he's the only man left." "His partner? Do you mean his Designated Hitter? Are there two of them out there or what?" "Well, it's like this ..." And so it went, confusion compounding confusion, for the next three hours; it was not one of the world's more successful cultural exchanges. In fact, the discussion threatened to become as long as a cricket match itself – and they can last for up to five days.

Back at the bar, the word was out that Matt Molloy would not actually be playing tonight; he'd just come back from a music festival at the island of Inishbofin and had a hangover the size of Mweelrae Mountain. "I walked past him in the street this afternoon," one of the Westport men told Matt's wife as she pulled the pints, "and I don't think he remembered who I was." "Don't worry about it," she said; "he didn't even recognize me when he got home last night." But the musicians who did play were nothing short of superb – a fiddle player and an accordionist, with some brilliant back-up playing by a bouzouki player. The bouzouki came from Greece into traditional Irish music sometime during the 1960s; with its clear, bright tone, its ringing trebles and its loud volume, it quickly established itself as the perfect instrument to send a session into flight. Together, they ripped through the reels with a dazzling display of speed and skill, filling the room with energy and excitement. They were fast and they were flawless – not the kind of people you would want to play with if you had a hangover, not even if you were Matt Molloy himself.

About half-way through the evening, an older man with horn-rimmed glasses managed to find a space next to me and set a glass of lemonade down on the table. He introduced himself as Mick Lavelle, singer and story-teller, from down the road in Westport. And at the first break in the music, he seized the moment and started to sing. Mick is the only singer I've encountered who runs songs together, in the same way that the musicians run reels together; once he's got the attention of the room, he sees no reason why he should let it go. He sang "The Drunk Driver," a parody of "The Wild Rover" ("I've been a Drunk Driver for many's a year, and I've spent all my money on whiskey and beer"), and followed it up immediately with "The Millionaire," about a man who wins the lottery, goes wild ("I headed for the local, sure I was feeling great; and friends I never knew I had came in to celebrate"), only to brought back to Earth by a sharp elbow in his side – his wife waking him up, calling him a raving lunatic, and ordering him to get out of bed and milk the cows. "'Twas lovely while it lasted," he wound up, "that winning dream of mine."

"I used to be a heavy drinker," he told me, as he sipped on a glass of lemonade, "but not any more; I'm a teetotaller now." What made him drink? "When I was young, I was very shy," he said, "and that's where the drink came in. Now that I'm old, I'm bold, but it's too late."

I asked him for a story, and he said he'd tell one if he felt the mood was right; you couldn't battle against Americans and Australians attempting to unravel the mysteries of baseball and cricket. But eventually, when the musicians had come up for air and the complexities of cricket had temporarily stunned the Americans into silence, things quietened down, and Mick stood up for a story:

Some of you people here might not know this, especially the people who are here on their holidays. But there was a time, a long time ago, when there were no looking glasses in Ireland. Now, you're probably asking yourselves, well then what did the ladies do? A good question. And the answer's quite easy. They would wait for a clear day, walk down to the river, and see their reflections in a clear pool of water. You didn't know that, now, did you?

Well one day, Dinny Noonan came down from Belmullet, a place so backward, so remote, that the men couldn't count their toes with their fingers. And here, in a shop in Westport, he saw a whole row of things he'd never seen before, and didn't he go up to them to give them a closer inspection. "By Jaysus," says he, looking at one straight in the face, "isn't that picture the picture of my very own father, and him dead these past ten years." "Where'd you get these?" he asks the shopman. "They come in from England," says he. "Well that's a queer thing," says Dinny, "and me never knowing me da was such a famous man in England. What would you be asking for them?" So he bought one for threepence, and carried it home with him, safe in his trouser pocket. And he'd pull it out every day, and take a good look at it, just to remind himself of his own father. But he thought it best to keep it from the missus, d'ye see, since she and the father had never been too taken with each other, and it would be best to let sleeping dogs lie.

Now, it didn't take long before the wife began to get her dander up. There was Dinny, back from away, sneaking squints into his pocket whenever he thought she wasn't looking. She began to fear the worst: he'd found some Fancy Woman in Westport, and was so smitten with the hussy that he couldn't go fifteen minutes without feasting his eyes on her. She'd get to the bottom of this, all right.

Now, one night there was a terrible fire three houses down the street, and all the men rushed out in their pyjamas to put it out before all Belmullet burned down. And that was her chance. She fished into his trouser pocket, and what did she pull out but the face of all her fears – the picture of the Westport Hussy. "And she's no oil painting, either," she said to herself as she snapped it in her purse.

Well, after that they fought like man and wife, till the air was thick with curses and you couldn't see the door for all the feathers flying – she with murder and mayhem on her mind, he telling her it was only his old da, and she never did like him anyway, and him famous in England. But if there was one man in the village who could settle the matter, that very man was the priest himself. For wasn't he educated in Maynooth itself, and hadn't he seen as much of the world as a decent man could be allowed to see?

So, they knocked on his door and went into his house and told him their different stories. There was only one thing for it; the priest himself must see the picture, and whoever he said it was, then that's who it must be. He looked at it long and hard. He looked at it sideways, and he looked at it lengthways. He looked at the front, and he looked at the back. And then he started to smile. And then he started to laugh. And he turned to the husband, and told him that was never a picture of his old da. And he turned to the wife, and told her that was never a picture of the Fancy Woman from Westport. And he turned to them both, and told them they were a right pair of eejits, if ever eejits there were.

"Would yous ever catch yourselves on and see sense?" he said. "Isn't that nothing else but a picture of the old parish priest who was here before me?"

The fiddle player drew his bow across the strings, the noise level picked up again, the music came dancing out of the session, and a steady stream of lemonade began to flow from the bar to Mick's table. Like a jig, like a reel, like a hornpipe, the story would be told many times, but it would never be told in quite the same way again.

That was the Tuesday. On the Wednesday morning, I walked along the streets of Westport and wandered in and out of the cafés and shops. And then, at a bridge down by the river, I came across a bust of John MacBride, native son and revolutionary hero. "No man can claim authority to barter away the immutable rights of nationhood," ran the plaque. "For Irishmen have fought, suffered and died in defence of those rights. And thank God Irishmen will always be found to snatch up the torch from the slumbering fire, to hold it aloft as a guiding light, and to hand it on, blazing afresh, to the succeeding generations." Stirring words, indeed; and words that he himself acted on, when he strode out with Patrick Pearse in the Easter Rising of 1916, fought for an Irish Republic, and faced the firing squad on the fifth of May – another martyr for old Ireland, another murder for the crown.

They knew that they would die, those men, but they believed that in their death would come new life, the life of a truly independent, united, Irish-speaking Ireland. "Do not remember my failures," Pearse had written, "but remember this my faith." When the rebels proclaimed the Irish Republic in 1916, they had little popular support; people spat on them in the street after they'd been taken prisoner. But when the British executed them – shooting Joseph Plunkett the day after his prison wedding to Grace Gifford, strapping the wounded James Connolly to his chair to face his death – feelings began to change. After all, when push came to shove, they were "our" boys, and you couldn't argue with their idealism, or forget the faith that made them lay down their lives for their country. You had to admire them for that.

Or had you? Where does courage end and fanaticism begin? Pearse was obsessed with death and dying, gripped by a lust for blood. "The last six months," he declared in 1915, reflecting on the carnage of trench warfare, "have been the most glorious in the history of Europe. It is good for the world that such things should be done. The old heart of the earth needed to be warmed with the red wine of the battlefields. Such august homage was never before offered to God as this, the homage of millions of lives given gladly for love of country." There were lessons here for Ireland: "We may make mistakes in the beginning and shoot the wrong people," he wrote; "but bloodshed is a cleansing and a sanctifying thing, and the nation which regards it as the final horror has lost its manhood."

But if it was fanaticism, was it necessary fanaticism? Was there no other way? The Irish Home Rule Party had already secured a significant degree of independence for the twenty-six counties outside the Protestant-dominated northeast, in legislation that would go into effect after the war. And when the smoke had cleared after all that sacrifice, all that suffering, all those rare times for death and Ireland, the settlement of 1921 that emerged from the revolution turned out to be substantially the same as the one that the Home Rule Party had worked out before the war. The ideals of a united, republican, Gaelic Ireland had run headlong into the realities of Protestant resistance, British power, and the English language. The Anglo-Irish Treaty of 1921 provoked a civil war between the idealists who stood by the principles of the Easter Rising and the pragmatists who settled for what they could get; the civil war claimed even more lives than the fight against Britain, and has scarred Irish politics ever since.

And so, I felt distinctly uneasy as I stood by the bust of John MacBride and read his words about passing the torch of revolution from generation to generation. For a quarter of a century now, that torch has been in the hands of the IRA, and the fire has burned thousands of people, including many of those who have been carrying the flame. Like the rebels of 1916, the IRA have been fighting a war that the vast majority of people on the island of Ireland do not want; like the rebels of 1916, the IRA have drawn sustenance from the conviction that their fight would be retroactively justified, once the Brits had been pushed out and the Prods had caved in. The idealism, the mystique of violence, and the glorification of the blood sacrifice that permeated the Easter Rising have all continued to inspire the IRA in their attempt to complete the "unfinished business" of 1916. The IRA claimed to be the true heirs of the Rising, and in this they are surely right. The results so far: a death toll of well over three thousand, a deeply divided society, and a war that no one has been able to win. No thanks; I want no part of such a revolution.

West along the Road

The mountain of Croagh Patrick rises over the sea like a myth. Long ago, on the road from Westport to Louisburgh, St Patrick climbed the mountain that is higher than all the mountains that face the setting sun, and fasted for forty days and forty nights. Mighty demon-birds whirled and wheeled around him, until he could see neither sky nor sun, neither the land beyond nor the land below. But he carried with him St Brigid's bell, which he rang at the birds and flung at the birds, until they scattered over the sea as far and as wide as the eye could reach and drowned themselves in the deep. And Ireland was free from demons for seven years and seven months and seven days.

Then the medieval chroniclers came, with their pens and their scrolls and their gowns, and walked through the land that had no snakes, the land that had no demons, the land where stories turned and twisted into each other like brambles and roses. And they listened and they learned, and they twisted and they turned, and they told the world their story, about how St Patrick and St Brigid's bell had driven the snakes out of Ireland.

This is still a place to cast out demons, a place to scatter evil spirits to the sea, a place for pilgrims. They came here long before the Christians came, for the Festival of Lughnasa that celebrated the beginning of the harvest in the Celtic calendar. They came here for centuries, on the last Sunday of each July, walking barefoot over rocks and stones that would blister the bones, until they reached the top and took the Black Bell of St Patrick, and passed it around themselves three times in the direction that the Sun passed around the Earth. And they come here still, carrying lanterns through the darkness, upward curves of pointed light, beacons of hope in the blackness. When it was over, there would be eating and drinking and music and dancing into the dawn, a celebration of life rising like the Sun into a new day.

From Croagh Patrick, I travelled on towards Louisburgh, following the route of that other Patrick, the Patrick Lynch who came here almost two hundred years ago to collect songs for Edward Bunting's *Ancient Melodies of Ireland.* "I found a blind piper near Louisborough," he reported in the summer of 1802, "who had the greatest variety of songs, tunes, and genuine poems, of any I ever met." The piper would have sung and played and read his poems at the post-pilgrimage sessions, where other musicians learnt from his tunes and taught him their own – words and music ringing briefly through the darkness, chasing the demons out to sea, words and music that were saved by a chance encounter with an itinerant collector.

I had a chance encounter myself on the road to Louisburgh, but not with a blind piper. As I was looking back on Croagh Patrick, lost in thought, a ruddy-faced man in a pre-Christian suit appeared from behind a farmgate and called me over. "I'm the lord of all the lands you can see," he said, laughing long and loud, and asking me where I was from. "Canada, is it? Well, let me tell you this: I know more professors in the universities from Canada than I do farmers from Mayo. McGill, Queen's, McMaster, I know them all. They'd come to me, you see, and I'd polish them off." I shifted uneasily on my feet. "You'd polish them off? And where would you do that?" "Harvard Medical School," he said; you'd have to suspend a hell of a

lot of disbelief to go along with that one. "Harvard Medical School? And what did you do there?" I asked, beginning to wonder if I was talking to a thinly repressed scalpel slasher. "I taught Americans how to jog," came the triumphant reply. Ah yes, the Harvard Medical School Jogging Program, run, so to speak, by a mad Mayo farmer who looked as though he had trouble enough leaning on his gate. At least he wasn't having fantasies about surgery. "I'm the one who started it all," he continued; "and look how well it's turned out. There's not an American you meet today who doesn't know how to jog – not even the president himself. He was my best student, you know." It was time to leave. "Two miles every other day, at eight minutes a mile," he called out as I cycled away. "That'll optimize your aerobic capacity. And don't forget your warm-down, or the Galactic Acid will get you. Bye now."

And so, wondering what kind of Galactic Acid he was on, I reached Louisburgh and turned south through the valley that winds through the Murrisk Mountains. A swift-running stream flowed into a long lake, as dark as the steep slopes pressing down upon it from either side. Beside the lake, on the narrow strip of land between road and mountain, you could see occasional traces of abandoned cottages, where people like Patrick Lynch's blind piper once lived.

Further along, there was a plaque with the words DOOLOUGH TRAGEDY, 1849, commemorating the Famine victims who died by this lake while returning from the local workhouse, after an unsuccessful attempt to get relief. The people who clustered around these valleys, like three million of their fellow Irish men and women, had existed on potatoes, usually around twelve to fourteen pounds a day. In 1845 the potato was hit by blight, and the crop failed for four years in a row; the staple diet of more than a third of the population disappeared, virtually overnight. By the time it was over, one million people had died of hunger and disease, and another million had emigrated; the country would never be the same again.

"The Almighty sent the potato blight," argued the revolutionary nationalist John Mitchel shortly after it was over, "but the English created the Famine." He pointed to the fact that the government allowed grain to be exported from the country while the people were starving, and that the relief measures were hopelessly inadequate. "The Irish fornicated themselves to death," wrote a modern historian, arguing that the lack of population restraint culminated in a Malthusian cataclysm when the land could no longer support the people.

And yet, the view that the Irish were responsible for their own fate ignores the fact that they were trapped in an economic system not of their own making, and forgets that the rate of population growth was already slowing down before the Famine. In many ways, contrary to the stereotype, the Irish were simply unlucky; the potato blight took everyone by surprise and was by no means inevitable. Had it not happened, the population would probably have declined gradually, without the trauma of the Hungry Forties. Once the blight did occur, though, and occurred four years in a row, famine was unavoidable; the hard fact was that there was not enough food to go round. There was nothing artificial about that.

But more, much more, could have been done to help the situation; British lethargy and British callousness cost countless lives that could have been saved. Relief measures were inconsistent and inadequate. By July 1847 the government had organized soup kitchens that fed three million people a day – a remarkable achievement for its time, even though the conditions in which the food was distributed were often demeaning. But instead of keeping this effort going, the government pulled out of the program later that summer and threw the responsibility for relief back on the Irish themselves. The Irish poor law system buckled, and then collapsed, under the strain. Meanwhile, the landlords, hit on one side by lack of rents and on the other by British demands that they shell out for relief, tried to stave off bankruptcy by mass evictions of tenants. A deep anger towards Irish landlordism and British indifference became riveted in the popular consciousness – making the genocidal interpretation of the Famine that much more believable.

Still, the charge of genocide – in the sense of premeditated mass murder, of a deliberate desire to extinguish the Irish people – does not hold up. The men who governed Ireland were good nineteenth-century Christians, not mass murderers in the style of Hitler, Stalin, or Pol Pot. And they generally saw the Famine as an Act of God –

a view that many Irish people themselves shared. Above all, the British government was trapped by the tyranny of an idea – the belief in *laissez-faire*, the notion that things would ultimately work out for the best if you didn't interfere with the natural operations of the economy. In the context of the Famine, though, a doctrinaire adherence to free market ideology could be nothing other than disastrous. "You cannot," wrote an exasperated official on the ground in Ireland, "you cannot answer the cry of want by a quotation from political economy."

And there's another side to this, as well. In the summer of 1846 it wasn't only the British government that allowed grain exports to proceed, some three months before the emergency grain imports from the United States were due to arrive. Prosperous Irish Catholic farmers and traders were also opposed to any restrictions on the export of grain – their grain – from the country; the traders even threatened to refuse to handle the emergency imports if they weren't allowed to continue the export trade. And it wasn't only Anglo-Irish landlords who evicted their tenants; Irish Catholic farmers also cleared their own land. Many of these same farmers protested at the cost of relief works; in some places, they made sure that their own sons profited from relief programs designed to help the people who were in desperate and immediate need. If you're looking at blame, you've got to look inside as well as outside Irish society.

The road remains silent here; the mountains brood in the bleakness and the lake reflects the stillness of the sky. Slowly, almost imperceptibly, the shadows shift, and shafts of sunlight break into the darkness of the valley. Soft purples stir in the sun – wild rhododendrons, mingling with the fading gold of gorse and the gentle red of the first fuchsia, shoots of beauty rising up from stony ground. The valley takes you down to the narrow sea inlet that separates the Murrisk and the Maamturk Mountains, where the road clings to the edge of the Killary fjord, and then turns eastwards to Aasleagh Falls.

The Erriff River rushes over the rocks like a fiddler rushing through a reel, but the sound is as soothing as a slow air. I wheeled the bicycle to the water's edge and played "The Rocks and the Water" on the whistle – the wistful theme tune of the whimsical film *Local Hero* – while the notes furled over the spray like wisps of cloud on a warm day. And then an Appalachian mountain reel, "Over the Waterfall," jumped into mind, bright and lively and buoyant, like a salmon in the stream. It stayed with me for the rest of the day, carrying me along the far side of the fjord, down towards the Connemara coastline.

This is a place of stark bogland and worn-down stone, a strange desert surrounded by distant mountains. I cycled past the long lake by the Letterfrack road, through the dark green tunnel of a forest, and into open spaces of wilderness and sky where cloud-printed patterns constantly change the colour and contours of the land. The Pins of Connemara came into view, quartzite peaks leaning awkwardly against the eastern sky, as the road circled past Ballynakill Bay and began its steep climb into Clifden.

At least it seemed steep, after the day's cycling. I was reminded of all those weight trainers I'd seen at the gym while preparing for the trip. They would begin by lifting impossibly heavy loads, and gradually decrease the weight until they were down to the lowest possible level; you would see men who were built like brick shithouses fighting for all they were worth just to benchpress twenty pounds. It had always seemed slightly insane to me; besides, I had enough trouble benchpressing twenty pounds to begin with. But whatever strength I may have had at the start of the day's journey had gone by the time I hauled myself up that hill on the road to Clifden.

The town was getting ready for its annual Arts Festival, the streets were full of backpacks and cameras, and itinerant writers and strolling musicians were staggering from bar to bar in syncopation. As I cycled through the main road, I had a strange, sun-induced hallucination: there, in the doorway of the Allied Irish Bank, stood the Laughing Cavalier, looking for the life of him as if he'd just stepped out of his own picture. I tried to think no more about it and travelled on to the Sky Road, where the sea-breeze softens the colours, and haystacks and stone walls and distant cliffs fade in and out of focus in the mist of the evening. And in a cottage overlooking the Atlantic, I settled in for the week.

Clifden was crackling with energy; the festival was pulling people into town, and the hostels were overflowing. At the bus-stop, a man who described himself as Tom the Poet was waiting for the next batch of tourists, in the hope that the "Garman garls," as he called them, would be irresistibly drawn to his literary credentials. And apparently, some of them were; his friends, who knew full well that the man couldn't tell a metonymy from a synecdoche, looked on the whole thing with a mixture of casual cynicism and deep jealousy. You'd see them walking down the street, shaking their heads and muttering to themselves in disbelief, while the Bard waited for the new faces coming in from Germany.

Everything in the festival was larger than life; exaggeration was the order of the day. The group that was playing in the Clifden Hotel that night was cheerfully billed as "America's top bluegrass band"; no one had ever heard of them before, and it turned out that one of the organizers had met them in a bar in Boston the previous summer and brought them over. The novelist Kazuo Ishiguro was there, reading from his latest book and playing some blues guitar on the side; no one could pronounce his first name, so he became known as Ish Ishiguro, as in Kris Kristofferson. When the news came through that his book had been shortlisted for the Booker Prize, the story quickly expanded to the point that he had actually won it, despite all his disclaimers. As things turned out, he actually did win it in the end – a tribute to the power of positive thinking in the Clifden Arts Festival.

I went over to Mannion's Pub, passing by the Allied Irish Bank in the process. The Laughing Cavalier had gone; but in his place was Little Red Riding Hood, looking surprisingly big and suspiciously in need of a shave. I moved on hurriedly to Mannion's, where Kevin Burke and Andy Irvine would be giving a concert that night. Kevin Burke is a superb fiddle player; he has had classical training, but doesn't let that get in the way of his traditional style. When he plays, he often looks bored out of his mind; but when you close your eyes and listen, you can feel the energy flowing through the music. Andy Irvine is a fine singer and a maestro of the mandolin, a man with fire in his fingers.

Their performance was wonderful, but what happened afterwards was better still. "Hang around here, in this room," a seasoned late-night drinker from Clifden advised me. I did, and sure enough, Kevin and Andy came in for a late-night session, released from the constraints of the concert. The barman started to pour free pints of Guinness – something that tended to enhance our enjoyment of the evening considerably. Kevin Burke and Andy Irvine, we decided in the true Clifden manner, were by far the greatest musicians in Ireland, possibly in the world.

It could have gone on all night, Kevin's increasingly intense playing and Andy's fingers flying all over the place, free pint after free pint. But, around four in the morning, there was a brief lull in the music while Andy decided to catch up with his drink. Seizing the moment, a German woman, who had somehow managed to evade the clutches of Tom the Poet, suddenly started to clear her throat. It was not a beautiful sound. "Oh, lie, the fields of Athenry," she sang, in harsh Teutonic tones, "where first I heard the small birds sing" – one of the worst songs in the country-and-Irish repertoire, now being performed determinedly off-key. I began to think that the ancient division of music into three categories needed revising: there was music that would make you sleep, music that would make you weep, and music that would make you leap, and then there was music that would make you run like hell. Our shoulders hunched together; we cringed over our beer, waiting for it to end. "That was very nice," someone said, after she had finished the song by repeating the chorus six times in a row. It was a fatal politeness. Thus encouraged, she proceeded to destroy "The Black Velvet Band" – a song that doesn't need much destroying in the first place. After that, there was was no dissuading or distracting her; she was set for the night.

Then she took the bodhrán out. Kevin looked at Andy; Andy looked at Kevin. And at this point, I learned something else about the two men – they could drink even faster than they could play. An entire table of alcohol was drained in the beat of a bar. "Well, that's us for the night," said Andy; "we're away to bed." They promptly disappeared through the door, and, it was credibly reported, were never to be seen in Clifden again.

I rose the next day with a great headache, feeling stupid as a mill-horse. To soothe the senses, I went to an afternoon harp recital in a pub courtyard, where Jan Harbison was playing. You don't often see the harp in pubs; traditionally, the instrument has been beyond the financial reach of most musicians, and the harpers generally needed aristocratic patrons to survive. Besides, it's difficult to carry around. But Jan stuffs the instrument into her aging Morris Minor, crams in a friend or two as well, and travels around the country playing her music at formal concerts, folk festivals and shebeens, anywhere and everywhere. Here, in the courtyard, "Miss MacLeod's Reel" reverberated against stone walls, shaded with moss and softened by geraniums. And then, a dark and mournful air that the harper Ruaidhrí Dall Ó Catháin composed some four hundred years ago, one of the earliest surviving pieces in the repertoire.

As she played, an ancient description of Irish harp music came to mind, from the writings of Gerald of Wales during his twelfth-century tour of the country. In general, he was unimpressed by the place; the Irish, he thought, were a bunch of barbarians, beyond the outer rim of civilization. But when it came to the music, he felt he was entering a different world:

I find among these people commendable diligence only on musical instruments, on which they are incomparably more skilled than any nation I have seen. Their style is ... quick and lively; nevertheless the sound is smooth and pleasant. It is remarkable that, with such rapid fingerwork, the musical rhythm is maintained and that, by unfailingly disciplined art, the integrity of the tune is fully preserved through the ornate rhythms and the profusely intricate polyphony – and with such smooth rapidity, such unequal quality, such discordant concord.

The harps in those days were very different; they had brass strings and they were played with long fingernails. As members of a caste apart, harpers devoted their lives to their art and were rewarded with a privileged place in Celtic society; they'd have been given Rolls-Royces, not Morris Minors. The music they played was different, too, from a world long before jigs and reels, with a wildness and beauty that we can only glimpse in fragments. But, for all that, something has carried through into the present. Rapid fingerwork, ornate rhythms, intricate polyphony, a smooth and pleasant style

– it all sounds very similar to Jan Harbison's harp playing in a Clifden courtyard, some eight centuries later.

She took a short break, fortified herself with a glass of lager, and continued with the music of Turlough Carolan, the greatest of the harpers whose compositions have come down to us. If ever there should be a new religion in Ireland, Carolan should be its Spiritual Leader and his music its inspiration. He lived during the late-seventeenth and early-eighteenth centuries, at a time when the old Gaelic order was crumbling; his life and his music straddled the world that was passing and the world that was coming to be. He played for the ancient Irish families, and he played for the new landlords who were replacing them. His music was also a mixture of old and new; it combined traditional Irish airs with modern Italian influences, resulting in beautiful pieces like "Carolan's Concerto." In a sense, there was nothing unusual about this; Irish musicians have always been an eclectic group of people, drawing on a wide variety of traditions and making them their own. It makes the music live, gives it new energy, keeps the blood flowing swiftly; there is plenty of room for original Celtic music, Celtic fusion music, and even Celtic confusion music. Academics may

argue until the cows come home about what is traditional and what is not; if it sounds good, it sounds good. And Carolan's compositions sound very good indeed.

Whatever else you could say about the man, you couldn't accuse him of excessive modesty:

> From me is each tale most melodious,
> It is I have been honoured by women,
> I am first in the power of the fingers,
> The likes of me will never be seen again.

Carolan wrote that verse to himself in 1726; his biographers like to think that it was half in jest. He started to play the harp at the age of eighteen, after he had been totally blinded by smallpox. Many of the itinerant harpers were blind; music was often the only avenue open to them. His patron, Mary MacDermott Roe – one of those women who had honoured him – had him "placed" with a harper for three years of training. Then, when he was ready, she gave him a horse, a guide, some money, and sent him on the road.

Because he started to play relatively late in life, Carolan was not a brilliant performer. His strength lay in his compositions rather than his technique, in the power of the ear rather than the power of the fingers. "My eyes," he said on one occasion, "are transplanted into my ears." He would compose tunes for his patrons as he rode on horseback through the rough roads of Ireland, and play them when he arrived at their homes. The tradition of hospitality was even stronger then than it is now; wandering harpers would always find a welcome. Besides, turning a bard away was a risky business; the chances were that he would get his own back by blasting your name throughout the land, in a kind of revenge by ridicule.

In 1738 Carolan composed his last tune. After years of wild drinking sprees and wonderful music, he finally returned to the MacDermott Roe family, the place where he had started. "I have come here after all I have gone through," he said, "to die at home at last, where I got my schooling and my first horse." He rested, steadied himself with a drink, and played his "Farewell to Music" – a plaintive, heartrending tune, full of dark minor chords, with tones of anger and frustration and resignation. Then they led him upstairs to bed; a few days later, he died in his sleep.

But that wasn't quite the end of the story. Three decades after his death, Carolan's grave was opened and his skull was placed in the chapel wall of the MacDermott Roes. It was widely believed at the time that you could cure illness in general and epilepsy in particular by grinding nine pieces of a cranium into fine powder, dissolving the powder into a concoction of water and bitter herbs, and drinking a mouthful each morning until it was gone. If you left anything, the dead man would come after you, looking for the missing part of his head. Another option was to boil milk in the skull, and drink it until you were cured. The milk turned black from the fire, and, in the words of one observer, had a "very unpleasant appearance"; it probably didn't taste too good either. At any rate, Carolan's skull was increasingly used for medicinal purposes, and was gradually being whittled away, year by year, from the scrapings of the cranium.

Then, in 1798, it disappeared.

Nobody really knows what happened. According to one account, a mad Orangeman rode into town, shot the skull to smithereens, cursed all Papists, and high-tailed it off to Sligo as fast as hooves would carry him. To this day, you hear tales that the skull rests in an Orange Lodge in Belfast, where it has supposedly been incorporated into obscure and mysterious masonic rituals. In another version, it was sent to Sir James Caldwell – who just happened to suffer from epilepsy – for safe-keeping in his castle museum.

Paddy Tunney, the traditional singer who comes from the Castle Caldwell area, tells a story about a couple of musicians who went down to the vaults beneath the castle museum one All Souls' night to brew up some poteen. They were playing the fiddle and the flute, and warming themselves by the fire, when two dark figures emerged from the shadows. One was the ghost of a local fiddler who had drowned in the lake; he borrowed the fiddle and played more sweetly than anyone alive. The other had a long black cloak, with a hood where his head should have been. That still didn't stop him from requesting a tune from the fiddler, although it's recorded that he spoke in very low voice. The poteen brewers didn't know which way was up and which way was down; it was weeks before they were sober again. And when they were, and when they realized that it was the ghost of Carolan they had seen, they were furious with themselves. "Damn it, damn it," they cried; "if only we'd known! If only we could have got him to play the harp for us!"

But Jan Harbison has her harp close beside her, her head is firmly on her shoulders, and she keeps the music alive. Back in Belfast, she helped organize the two-hundredth anniversary celebrations of the Belfast Harp Festival, which in 1792 gathered together some of the few remaining Irish harpers, in an attempt to "revive and perpetuate the Ancient Music and Poetry of Ireland." Among the performers at the festival was the mercurial and brilliant Rose Mooney, whose talent on the harp was only matched by her ability in consuming alcohol; she eventually drank herself to death with looted liquor during the Rebellion of 1798. All of the other players were men; they were generally well over fifty, and most were blind.

Only one of them, the ninety-seven-year-old Denis Hempson, still played in the old style, with long curled fingernails; this was music from a lost world, and it sounded foreign to eighteenth-century ears. Edward Bunting, in his efforts to save the music for future generations, had great difficulty in transcribing Hempson's tunes; they didn't correspond to contemporary norms. As for Hempson himself, he couldn't have cared less about posterity. There was no use in playing the old pieces, he said; they were too hard to learn, and they only brought back bad memories. Still, when all was said and done, the harp must have been good for his health. Denis Hempson was still playing after the age of a hundred, and actually lived in three centuries; he had been born in 1695, and kept going until 1807, when a barrel of beer finally got the better of him.

The Harp Festival of 1792 not only presented and preserved the ancient music; it also strengthened the identification of the Harp with the Nation. The United Irishmen, who met in Belfast while the festival was going on, adopted the "new-strung harp" as a symbol of national regeneration. And one radical Irish member of parliament, Sir Francis Dobbs, went even further. He pointed out in 1800 that the harp was the instrument of Ireland, and noted that linen was the country's native product. He went on to recall the story of St Patrick banishing the snakes from Ireland, and to remind his readers that the religious capital of the country was the town of Armagh. Then, pulling everything out of the hat at once, he came to his dazzling conclusion: Ireland was to be the site of the Second Coming. The angelic hosts, clothed in white linen, playing their heavenly harps, would naturally descend on Ireland, where the great serpent Satan had already been scotched. And could there be any doubt that Armagh was a modern corruption of the word Armageddon?

The last notes of Jan Harbison's harp faded into the afternoon, the courtyard slowly emptied, and we walked together along the streets of Clifden. Intense poets were reading introverted lines about lost love; a film crew was assembling around a group of increasingly self-conscious buskers; Tom the Poet was waiting at the bus-stop. Down the road, by the Allied Irish Bank, there was now a Human Tree – a face sticking out of a papier mache trunk, covered in a pastiche of branches and leaves. Dogs and drunken men approached it in desperation, but still it remained rooted to the ground, unbowed and unmoving.

In the evening, I was invited for dinner at the home of Brendan Flynn, the festival organizer. There were about a dozen of us there, dipping our spoons into vats of stew, supping from pitchers of punch, forming a circle of laughter around the table. We took turns in telling a story or singing a song, until we had gone around the table sunwise at least three times. And we heard it all that night. A man who had written some of the Irish Rovers' Greatest Hits started singing them himself; someone else retaliated with a series of Shel Silverstein songs, starting with "Don't Give a Dose to the One You Love Most," and going downhill from there. "The Unicorn," mercifully, remained conspicuous by its absence; even here, there were limits. We heard haunting airs sung in Irish, and we heard booming Orange toasts, delivered in Mock Paisley style: "To the Glorious, Pious, and Immortal Memory of King William the Third, and against Popes and Popery, Rogues and Roguery, Slaves and Slavery, Knaves and Knavery, brass money and wooden shoes." Boos and groans and laughter all round. And then an indignant rejoinder: "May he who rejects this toast be slammed, crammed, rammed and jammed into the muzzle of the Great Gun of Athlone, and the Gun fired into the Pope's belly, and the Pope fired into the Devil's belly, and the Devil fired into the Gates of Hell, with the key safe in an Orangeman's pocket." Shouts of Amen, Mighty Stuff, Grand Altogether; jovial reminders that we must cherish equally all the children of the nation; cheerful counter-toasts to the damnation of all Orangemen who had ever lived or were yet to be born; more wine, more stories, more songs.

At my turn, I tried to sing some poetic gems from the country-and-western repertoire: "I'll Get over You if I Have to Build a Bridge," "If You Keep Throwing Dirt at Me You'll Soon Start Losing Ground," "Drop-kick me Jesus through the Goalposts of Life," and the like. Each time I began, though, I was drowned out by hoots and hisses, and threatened with calls to cut off my alcohol supply. In the end, after an attempt to sing "I'm an Old Cowhand" in an upper-class English accent was shouted down, we settled for "Show Me the Way to Go Home" – the Verbose Variation:

> Indicate the route to my abode
> I am fatigued and I wish to retire;
> I imbibed an alcoholic beverage sixty minutes ago
> And it travelled directly to my cerebellum.
> No matter where I perambulate
> Over terra firma, aqua terra or atmospheric vapour
> You will always hear me chanting this refrain,
> Indicate the route to my abode.

Shortly afterwards, I passed out.

The next morning was even more fragile than the last; a mental fog had enveloped me and an atmospheric depression began to settle on my brain. After scraping myself off the floor and drinking several mugs of black coffee, I set out along the Sky Road for the town school, the focus of the day's activities. There, in the play-ground, I saw Dracula standing by the swings, blood-red lipstick on his collar; by this time, nothing in Clifden seemed extraordinary any more. Inside, Brendan Flynn was looking cool and refreshed, with no visible effects from the previous night. He was organizing a series of discussion groups on everything from the art of writing (you start with a pen, and you wait) to the art of bodhrán making (you start with a goat, and you don't wait; after that, it gets rather messy). In one classroom, a scholar from England, who looked like he'd been around for several centuries, was happily tracing the origins of the Irish language back to the Garden of Eden, arguing that Adam and Eve spoke Gaelic, and putting in a modest claim for the Hibernian basis of all civilization. There were no prizes for guessing the language spoken by the Serpent.

Back in town, I tried to kick-start myself into action with the World's Largest Fry-Up, but it only made me feel queasier. "That's because you didn't eat enough of it," volunteered a friend, helpfully. I got the feeling that I'd better not stay in town much longer; my liver and my lungs were on the point of armed rebellion. But there was one more night to go, and I had just enough energy left to slump into a session at Griffin's Pub. At first, the musicians looked and sounded as knackered as I felt. Everything was in slow motion, and even the bluegrass band from Boston dropped down to thirty-three rpm (Old Style), as they struggled through Lester Flatt and Earl Struggs's "Foggy Mountain Breakdown." "Holy ga-moly, that was pretty goddam awful," said the mandolin player when they'd finished; "Flatt and Scruggs would turn in their graves." "They're not dead," replied the guitarist, wearily. "Well, they would be if they heard yous fellows," shot back a voice from across the bar. Unde-terred, they moved on to a hung-over version of the "Red River Valley"; more like the "Red River Vallium," growled the man at the next table.

Gradually, though, they picked up the pace, operating on the principle that the best cure for sleep deprivation was a gallon or two of Guinness – dubious in theory, but surprisingly effective in practice. To crank themselves into a higher gear, they started singing "Your Cheatin' Heart" and "Bobby McGee." I began to get alarming flashbacks from spit-and-sawdust bars in northern Ontario, where down-and-out country singers with beat boxes would sing the very same songs before the stripper came on and did unusual things with plastic snakes. Mercifully, the lads returned to the reels, and the image soon faded from mind. By the end of the evening, they were belting out the "Nine Pints of Roguery" and other brilliant tunes at breakneck speed. In a last gasp of life, I joined a bodhrán player for a set of jigs, driving them home at full throttle. And at that, I decided to pack it in for the night; it was a good note to leave on.

I was back on my bicycle, somewhat the worse for wear, by the middle of the next morning. As I circled through Clifden for the last time, Jan Harbison and Brendan Flynn called me over for a farewell coffee. We talked quietly for a while about coming back again next year, full of good intentions and promises that we meant to keep. Before I left, they introduced me to a man by the name of Thom McGinty, over at the bar; he was standing still as a statue and tall as a tree, wearing a red anorak and smiling like a vampire. I couldn't quite put my finger on it, but I could have sworn I'd seen him somewhere before.

A Trip
to Galway

I had originally planned to follow the coast road from Clifden to Roundstone, but both Brendan Flynn and last night's bodhrán player insisted that I take the Bog Road cutting across from Ballinaboy to Toombeola. "It's a mystical place," Brendan had said; "a road haunted with its own spirits." Far beyond fallen stone fences, dark pools of water reached out to solitary, storm-twisted trees, shaped by their search for shelter and light. Black buzzards flapped lazy wings above the water and moved slowly over their own reflections. A thin strip of asphalt, and distant, parallel turf-lines; these were the only signs of the world I had left. The road moved through croppings of rock, scattered like seeds by some giant hand. Here was softness and starkness; hues of heather in fields of stone, buttercups and butterflies breathing through the crevices, bees riding on the breeze. On the northern horizon, the Pins of Connemara collected the only clouds in the sky, clinging to each other for comfort. I found a sheltered seat formed by the rocks, facing the mountains, where the whistle could wail with the wind, and played "The Earl's Chair," a wild, lonesome reel, in this wild, lonesome place.

Further along, after Toombeola, the land briefly meets the sea, before the road carries you over the rockscape that tumbles down from Derryrush to Screeb. I cycled into the sun and into the wind, southwards into the *Gaeltacht* of Galway Bay. The Aran Islands appeared like long, low shadows before the horizon; Black Head and the cliffs of Clare evaporated into a distant shoreline. This would be a fine place to live, on these western shores with their summer sunsets, drinking all the day in old pubs where fiddlers play, singing songs for Ireland.

But before the pubs, there was the road to negotiate – and from Costelloe to Spiddal it is narrow, busy, and pot-holed beyond belief. You cling to the razor's edge of the road, while every motor vehicle in the world from tractors to tour buses shaves by you at terrifying speed. With white-knuckled terror, you grip the handlebars as tightly as you can, brushing against brambles and palpitating over pot-holes. There's absolutely no room to manœuvre; you just go in a straight line, hope for the best, brace yourself for the worst. And it was here, after bouncing in and out of a crater from the moon, that I was brought face to face with the most trying experience of my entire trip – a puncture.

Now, I have never been a very practical person; anything requiring manual dexterity with machines leaves me confused, perplexed, and frustrated. The writing was on the wall, or rather the report card, from an early age. I spent my entire first year of compulsory woodwork at school trying to make a clothes peg, while my friends were rapidly progressing to shoe racks and magazine racks and various other items that would impress

their doting parents. Mr Gom, the woodwork teacher, penned some unkind remarks after the obligatory F: "This boy sets himself an exceedingly low standard," he wrote, "which he consistently fails to come up to." But the truth of it was that I tried very hard; it was just that I was, well, hopeless. I still have that clothes peg; it is forced together at the joints, it looks slightly obscene, and it is too big for any coat tag that ever existed. Other than that, though, it's fine.

So there I was, on the Galway road, staring at my bicycle and wondering what to do. The puncture was on the back tyre, *of course*, the one with the chain and the gears; the Quest for the Holy Grail itself would be child's play compared with the Way to the Inner Tube. King Arthur only had dragons and monsters to contend with; I had wheelnuts welded into the bicycle frame. King Arthur had dozens of knights with him; there was only one of me. For the first seven days, I relied exclusively on exhortations, but gradually came to realize that not even the finest oratory in the world would have loosened those wheelnuts. For the next seven days, I went at them with the wrench, trying desperately to remember which direction tightened and which direction loosened. Finally, after turning them three times sun-wise, they came free.

Then there was the chain, thick black with as much grease as you'd find in an Ulster Fry. I peeled it from the sprocket, caking my hands with an oily grime that stuck to everything I touched. Out came the tyre levers, which kept bouncing back from the spokes into my face; after much grunting and groaning and cursing and swearing, I finally separated the tyre from the wheel, pulled out the entrail of the Inner Tube, and inspected it for portents of the future. But it was silent; it gave No Sign. I pumped air into it, and ran my hand over the surface to locate the leak. Still nothing; I needed to pump more air into the tube, put it in some water, and watch for the bubbles. Easier said than done; there was the sea, but the waves wouldn't cooperate, and the water was too cold to wade around in for long. In the end, I found a rockpool – and there, amid tiny crabs and sea anemones, I also found the leak.

The task now was to plug it. In theory, this should have been quite straightforward; you take a chalk pencil from the puncture repair kit, mark the leak, and patch it up. In practice, though, it

wasn't quite that simple. You could only locate the leak by immersing the tube in water. This, perhaps predictably, tended to make it rather wet. And you can't put chalk marks on a wet surface. But, being a resourceful kind of person, I took out my handkerchief, which immediately became covered with oily-black fingerprints, and wiped the tube dry. This would have been fine, except that by the time I'd finished, the precise position of the puncture was no longer clear. Bad memories of Snakes and Ladders came bubbling to the surface; you've got six squares to go, the end is in sight, and then you throw a three and slither down to the depths of despair. I was on the verge of throwing a two-year-old's temper tantrum. Whatever else this experience was, it was not character building.

And so, it was back to the rockpool to repeat the water test; only this time, I decided to keep my thumb on the puncture and let nature take its course. But this being Ireland, place of precipitation, it was not long before the black clouds began to drift in from the Atlantic. A gentle drizzle at first, something that would surely pass soon; and when it did pass, it was replaced by a Niagara Falls of a flood. I could not, in truth, say that this improved my mood; in fact, I became rather querulous, sitting with my thumb on a torn piece of rubber, shivering through a soaking on what was supposedly a summer's day. Unbidden questions began to enter my mind, like sharp stones piercing through protective layers of consciousness. Who built this pot-holed apology for a road in the first place? Why couldn't I be better at things mechanical? Who in their right mind would want to live in such a god-forsaken climate? I had found the Inner Tube, and I was not happy.

But in the end I got out the glue, most of which wound up on my fingers, fumbled it onto the patch, and slid the patch onto the tube. After waiting for it to set, I began the arduous task of reassembling the bicycle – working the tyre back onto the wheel, working the wheel back onto the bike, finding the wheelnuts that had mysteriously moved from the place where I had so carefully put them, realigning the gears, and balancing the brakes. By this time, Niagara Falls had passed down the bay to Galway, where they were so inured to the wetness that they probably wouldn't even bother opening their umbrellas. Still, I was beginning to feel better. This was a Trial, a Skill-Testing Experience, and even though it had taken a while, even though it had added a month and a day onto my trip, I had come through in the end. Take that, Mr Gom, I thought to myself as I remounted the bicycle; I may have failed woodwork, I may have been mechanically challenged, but when it came to the crunch, I had done it. "We Shall Overcome," I sang to myself as I continued east on the road to Spiddal.

Thirty seconds later, I came to an abrupt halt. It was the back tyre. It was flat again.

A few years ago, I heard a story about a Dublin singer who was performing in the recurring nightmare of Gilbert and Sullivan's *HMS Pinafore*. One night, singing

> I thought so little, they rewarded me,
> By making me the ruler of Queen's Navee,

for the millionth time, he suddenly stopped. "Fuck this for a game of soldiers," he said, and stomped off stage. I knew exactly how he felt. Namoore of this; from now on, I'd be hitch-hiking.

As it turned out, hitching with a broken-down bicycle was not nearly as difficult as I'd imagined. The key was to be selective; family cars were impossible and large lorries were improbable, but there was a fair chance that vans, open-backed trucks, and Volkswagon buses might stop. Besides, I'd developed quite a lot of experience at hitching over the years and had some emergency techniques to fall back on in times of crisis. One was to wait for the moment that your eyes met those of the driver, nod appreciatively as if he or she had signalled to stop, pick up your gear, and run after the car for all you were worth. You had to be reasonably fit, and you had to be prepared to make a right eejit out of yourself, but it was surprisingly successful. Sometimes, you could make the drivers think that they really had signalled to stop, and they would pull up out of a misplaced sense of guilt. More often, one of the drivers in the cars behind would stop out of sympathy, believing that the person ahead had been maliciously deceitful, had behaved like a right gobshite, building up your expectations, making you run like that for nothing.

There was another approach that was equally effective, but required less effort – dropping down on your knees in an attitude of prayer. And it was this one that did the trick, as a man in a grocery van pulled over and drove me into Spiddal. "This is the place for the music," he said as we turned off the main road and passed Tigh Hughes's pub on the right; "the finest sessions in the country, you'll find there." Tigh Hughes, he told me, was where one of Ireland's best traditional groups, De Dannan, started to play together. They go back a long time, play like magicians and wizards, and leave legendary sessions in their wake. "They are the most handsome and delightful company," ran one of their earliest reviews, "the fairest of form, the most distinguished in their equipment and apparel, and their skill in music and playing, the most gifted in mind and temperament that ever came to Ireland."

The driver dropped me off at the bed-and-breakfast up the road, where I parked the bicycle out of sight and out of mind, and spent an hour or so in the bathroom scrubbing oily tar from hands and fingers. When I'd cleaned myself up, I chatted for a while with Big Sean, the proprietor. There were many fine walks in Ireland, he said, but for his money the best one was just up the hill, where you could see all the islands of Galway Bay and the coast of Clare. It takes you along narrow roads and scrawny land, beyond the bungalow line, until you are alone in the wilderness, and the view expands with every upward step – Inishmore, Inishmaan, Inisheer, tourist-trampled fragments of a fading world; the cliffs of Moher, sheering into the sea; an eastering plain and a westering ocean; storm clouds to the south and a soft sky above. Here, at the end of a day that had been magical and maddening, was the stillness of the centre and the softness of the evening, a place of solitude and a place of peace.

Eventually, as day turned into night, I wandered back down the hill and turned from the wide open spaces to the tightly packed pub. In the corner, three lads were singing some of the folk classics and singing them well – "She Moved through the Fair," "Peggy Gordon," "Isn't It Grand, Boys, to Be Bloody Well Dead." One of them picked up a whistle and played in a dazzling, brilliant style, with ornamentations rolling effortlessly into ornamentations, in spirals of notes that would make your head spin with the speed.

But when I went to the bar for the customary pint of Guinness, I began to realize that something was not quite right. Normally, the sight of stout-on-draught pouring in the glass brings on an anticipatory thirst; this time, I felt my stomach rising with the bubbles. A serious Danger Signal: I couldn't bring myself to touch a drop. I tried to stay at the session, but soon realized that the consequences would be unpleasant and embarrassing; in fact, the sooner I got to a sink, the better. I belched my way back up the street to the bed-and-breakfast and staggered into the toilet. This was food poisoning with a vengeance, food poisoning aggravated by exhaustion, the accumulated exhaustion of too many late-night sessions and too much cycling, too many drinks and too little sleep. I spent the night in a one-way conversation with Twyford's Porcelain, trying to speak when there was nothing left to say, wretched and retching, retching and wretched, until morning came and I lay on my bed, scared to move for setting off the sickness again.

I stayed in that position for the next three days, sustained by the occasional sip of boiled ginger ale, and tried not to think of the sessions I was missing. Gradually, the heaviness began to lift, and I found that I was able to turn from side to side without having to rush back to the bathroom. The family members came in with slices of toast and cups of tea, and would talk about their life in Spiddal. "How long have you been here?" I asked, when I was finally able to talk again. "Our people have been here ever since Cromwell sent them," replied Big Sean – the Cromwellian clearances, when Catholic rebels in the seventeenth century were given the choice of Hell or Connacht, and wound up in places like this; the folk memories linger. "We all grew up thinking we were made for export," he said. "Before the war it was America, and then it was England." But the tourist trade gave them a new economic lifeline, reconnecting them with their home. "We knew things were changing," he told me, "when the people across the road put a 'HOTEL' sign outside their house, and the next morning the wee girl came out on the street calling 'Does anyone know what a scrambled egg is?'"

On the fourth day, I struggled out of bed, walked on unsteady feet through the village, and sat quietly by the sea. As I went back past An Crúiscín Lán, another of Spiddal's pubs, the sound of a reel drew me inside, despite myself. A bouzouki, whistle, and accordion were up against a wall of intoxicated French post-adolescents, away from home and mad for action; the musicians were putting up a valiant fight, but it was a losing battle. This is Tourist Hell, I thought to myself, still not in the best of moods. And I made two Rules of Travel for survival in the west of Ireland. Number One: Never stay in a town that has more than one Youth Hostel. And Number Two: Never eat funny-tasting cream with your apple pie when you stop at a roadside pub in Toombeola, on the road to Spiddal.

But, somehow, the tourist tide had passed by Tigh Hughes, where a fiddle player sat round the musicians' table with an accordionist and a guitarist. I pulled up a chair next to one of the Old Fellows in the place. He told me how he had worked in England for many years, and had retired to his native Spiddal, where he rides a battered old bicycle to and from the pub each day. "We're in the minority now," he said; "the tourists have taken over. But, that's the way of it." "Everything is faster now than it used to be," he continued. "The cars go faster, the bicycles go faster, the people go faster." And then he paused and laughed: "The energy goes faster, too, you know."

In my present condition, I knew only too well. When I started to learn the tin whistle, I bought an instruction book by Geraldine Cotter – the "Traditional Irish Tin Whistle Tutor," it was called. There were a couple of instruction records attached, the kind that are made of bendable plastic, specially designed to destroy your stylus in a second. Through the static, you could hear Geraldine Cotter play each piece at a slow and easy speed, to get you into the way of playing it. "And here it is again," she would then say, "at a faster pace" – at which point she sprinted through the tune quicker than Ben Johnson ran the hundred metres, and he on steroids as well. I'd been playing faster than I was capable, the notes were slurring into each other, and the breath was running short. It was time to slow things down for a while, to get more than six hours' sleep a night, to cycle less than sixty miles a day.

I had, at any rate, decided to get back on the bicycle. The more I thought about it, the more hitch-hiking across Ireland with a bike seemed cumbersome and crazy. And so, the next day, I bought a new inner tube, and even managed to install it without sending my blood pressure through the roof. After an early night and a late morning, I was back on the Galway road, still feeling sluggish, in the teeth of a strong east wind. But I didn't have far to travel, and by the early afternoon I was browsing through the bookshops and hanging out in the cafés of Quay Street, taking life easy.

Slowly, over the next few days, my energy returned. But then it's hard not to be energetic in Galway; the place is bursting with traditional music and the streets are teeming with brilliant buskers – a young woman with a whistle on one corner, a trio playing fiddle, flute, and bodhrán on another, and an Irish tenor down the street who would put John McCormack to shame. In almost every pub, there's a session going on, musicians huddling around crowded tables, the air thick with noise and smoke. At Taaffe's, a melodeon player pierced through the haze of conversation with sharp-edged reels; before long, a fiddle player materialized out of the crowd, and more musicians followed. The magic ring expanded across the room, enchanting everyone it touched.

Further down the road, at Tigh Neachtain – the House of Neachtain, the best traditional music pub in the city – a back room session was in full swing, with the feet of a dancer providing the rhythm.

But this was a different kind of dancer – a wooden doll, wearing a suit of clothes and dancing shoes, with arms and legs that swung freely, and joints at the knees and elbows. You inserted a short pole into the dancer's back and placed him on a plywood springboard lodged between your thigh and your chair, sticking out towards the table. Then you tapped the springboard with one hand, and bounced the dancer on it with the other; before you knew it, he was rattling away like a real step dancer on a flagstone floor. I'd seen this kind of thing before in the United States, where they are called limberjacks, but I'd never seen one played so well. The dance master made his puppet match the music, with contrapuntal rhythms and variations in volume; and for extra effect, he could make the arms swing back and forth when the music really started to fly.

Tigh Neachtain became my musical home for the next few days. It's not a place for the claustrophobic, but the crack is mighty, as they say. Breda Smyth and Vinny Kilduff played the whistle so well that I was torn between practising twelve hours a day, or simply throwing the thing into Galway Bay and giving up for ever. Maureen Fahy played crisp, clean, and quick reels on the fiddle, while Brian Lennon punched out tunes on the flute; the pub attracts the best traditional musicians in the country. There were some interesting instruments as well; Pádraig Ó Carra played a few solo pieces on the zither, a horizontal wire-strung lap harp that came to Ireland from Europe and enjoyed a brief period of popularity around the turn of the last century, before fading out of sight and sound.

One of Pádraig's best pieces was a slow air called "The Bonny Bunch of Roses." The tune goes back to time immemorial, but it was first set to English words during the Napoleonic Wars, when many Irish people came to see Bonaparte as their political saviour. He was the Green Linnet, flying over the country with freedom on his wings, carrying the hope of liberation from English rule. In the song, a young "native of Erin" encounters a beautiful and mysterious Empress – the female personification of Ireland – on the banks of the Rhine:

> In soft accents she cried, O my linnet so green
> Sweet Boney, will I e'er see you more?

But Bonaparte had left the river for the east, with the largest army
the world had ever seen:

> He took three hundred thousand men
> And kings likewise to bear his train,
> He was so well provided for,
> That he could sweep the world for gain.
> But when he came to Moscow
> He was overpowered by the sleet and snow
> With Moscow all a-blazing
> And he lost the bonny bunch of roses-o.

The bonny bunch of roses was England, Scotland, Wales, and Ireland; the Irish dream of Napoleonic deliverance had been broken
on the steppes of Russia.

Or so it seemed. The hard truth was that Napoleon was more
interested in conquest than liberation, in turning Ireland into a
puppet that would dance to any tune he called. Had Napoleon won,
the Irish would have simply exchanged one form of colonialism for
another. The dream only fed false hope to a defeated people; in the
end, the Irish who wanted independence would have to rely largely
on themselves, although not on themselves alone.

The metallic notes of the melody rang through the room, aching
like a song of lost love. But the lament was followed, in true session
style, by a wild exuberance of jigs and reels, as if purging the place
of sadness. There were many tunes that I'd never heard before,
along with the more familiar ones that had everyone joining in,
raising the volume and lifting the spirit – "The Virginia Reel" and
"The Galway Rambler," carefree and joyful and lively and vibrant,
tunes that you lose yourself in, tunes that make you sway in your
seat. We finished the night with "The Tarbolton Set," three reels
that Michael Coleman had recorded together back in 1934 and that
have remained in the repertoire ever since. You just let yourself go,
let the notes find themselves, forget about punctures and food
poisoning and false hopes, and float as freely as a leaf on a stream,
or a bicycle sailing across a Bog Road on a soft summer's day.

From Here to Clare

Three roads wind their separate ways through the north Clare countryside, leading towards mystery, marriage, or music. The first runs from Ballyvaughan into the Burren, a wilderness of limestone where otherworlds collide and combine. There are ancient corals from an ancient sea, and there are wildflowers from the Mediterannean, specks of red and purple and blue in a desolate rockscape. There are fairy forts in rings that grow out of the ground, and there are dolmens that are disguised by their stone-strewn surroundings and that carry cryptic messages from the Celtic past – "D and G were here," carved on every prehistoric tomb in the country.

If you backtrack to Ballyvaughan, you can opt instead for the road that leads to marriage, the road to the match-making fair of Lisdoonvarna. Here, you can fall in love for the night to the country-and-Irish music of Big Tom, and listen to pick-up lines the likes of which will not be heard again – approaches ranging from the monosyllabic ("Dance") to the baroque ("Would you like to come to the cemetry with me tomorrow morning to help me put flowers on me granny's grave?"). And if you should tire of Big Tom, you can always go across the road to the pub where a traditional group billed as Tír na nÓg – "Land of Youth" – was playing. In keeping with the spirit of the fair itself, Tír na nÓg represented the triumph of wishful thinking over objective reality; the median age of the musicians was somewhere around ninety-seven. "How did you get your name?" I asked them during one of their frequent breaks. "Well, it seemed a good idea at the time, when we first started up," said one. "How long ago was that?" "Now, let me think," he replied; "I'd say it would have been the summer before last."

But my quest was for the Land of Music, the road that takes you through west Clare to Doolin and Miltown Malbay. Until recently, you wouldn't have been able to find Doolin on the map; twenty years ago, it consisted of little more than a few scattered houses and two pubs that happened to have the best music and crack in the country. The late great Miko Russell played his whistle, the hospitality flowed with the reels, the laughter came easily, the nights never ended. Little by little, the word got out: this was the one place that should never be missed, the Celtic experience of a lifetime. Doolin had become the Mecca of Traditional Music.

And so, more and more people came – from Germany, from America, from France, from Australia, from anywhere and everywhere. But they couldn't be sure that they would get to hear the music, given the spontaneity of the sessions; people who had travelled thousands of miles for a three-week holiday might spend half the time cooling their heels and waiting for something to happen. So it made sense to bring in paid musicians, who would guarantee regular sessions and draw in still more players and listeners; the reputation of Doolin grew, and still more people came. But they needed places to stay, and there were not enough bed-and-breakfasts to go round. So it made sense to build youth hostels for the visitors; at the last count, there were three of them, with rooms for more than two hundred people. But they found that the pubs were too small, and that they were crammed together

past the point of comfort. So it made sense to knock down a few walls and build extensions that would cope with the crowds.

The result? The publicans came to enjoy some well-earned prosperity, and the musicians came to earn some much-needed money. And the original character of Doolin, with its wonderful warmth and charm and vitality and music, had been eroded beyond recognition. The last time I was there, the waitress was being rude to a group of German tourists, and an American at the bar was singing an a cappella version of "Sweet Baby James" in a voice that sounded like scratched nails on sandpaper. Whatever else it was, it was no longer the home of traditional music; the place had become a victim of its own success.

By way of relief, I cycled on down to Doolin Point and waited for the tides to turn and the boat to come in for the trip to Inisheer, the easternmost of the Aran Islands. It was one of those rare, calm days of mist and sunshine, a day when you couldn't imagine the winds being strong or the waves being wild. Even on the crossing itself, it was so still that people were able to light cigarettes for each other without cupping the matches behind their hands; "there's only one day in a century when you can do that," said one of the crew members, who looked old enough to know. A tune came to

mind, a beautiful slow air written by another traveller who made this journey – "Inisheer," named after the island itself. It fitted the day and it fitted the place; it brought a sense of peace, of oneness with nature, of belonging.

Yet I didn't really belong here; none of us did. Tens of thousands of visitors make this trip each summer, and the area around the harbour is geared to catering for us, like nets waiting for shoals of fish. Walking along the road by the beach, I began to feel like an intruder, a spectator from another world; it was as if the tourists were here to see exotic specimens in a zoo, and the islanders were going to get what they could while the getting was good. I began to fear that we were slowly turning Inisheer into another Doolin.

The feelings began to abate as I moved further from the harbour, into the land of stone-fenced farms and narrow paths beyond the bay, but they did not disappear. After a while, lost in thought and a labyrinth of trails, I came across an old man working in the small square of a field. He wore one of those ancient, all-purpose black suits, and he was carrying a barrel of water by a rope over his shoulder. I gave him the Ulster nod; he gave me the Connacht wave of the hand and said something to me in Gaelic. "I'm sorry," I said, "but I don't speak a word of Irish." "Well, it's a terrible thing when people don't know the language of their own country. Are you walking far?" "Until the sea." "You're a very fit looking young fellow," he said, lowering the barrel of water from his back; "how old are you?" I gave him a rough approximation of my age, and he asked me for a rough approximation of his own. Eighty-five, I suggested. "Isn't it something," he said, neither confirming nor denying the figure, "isn't it something for a man of my age to be carrying such a heavy load?" I could only agree that it was. "You look like a strong young lad." And then the barrel hit the ground, right on cue.

"Would you like me to help you with that?" "Oh no, not at all; you go on and enjoy your walk now." "I don't mind; I'd be happy to help out." "No, no, there's no reason for you to do that; it's a lovely day to be sitting by the sea, instead of hauling an old barrel around." "No really, I don't mind," I said, pulling the barrel up by the rope and forcing it over my shoulder. "Well, now, that's very good of you." "No problem."

Only it was a problem, a big problem. Because far from being a strong young lad, I'm one of the weakest men in the western hemisphere. My legs are all right – the cycling has seen to that – but my upper body is a muscle-free zone, with a concave chest, and arms that can lift only one pint of Guinness at a time. In the instant that I got the barrel over my shoulder, I lurched sideways like a ship's mast suddenly struck by a force ten gale, and started staggering across the field while the searing pain of rope cut through raw flesh. "Just down the road a bit, that's all," he said, as I crumpled into the ground. The man was good, there was no doubt about it; he'd played on my guilt, my pride, my eagerness to please, and without so much as asking a question he'd got me under a barrel. If he'd been born in New York, he'd have wound up as a multimillionaire used-car salesman, all smiles and handshakes and you don't realize you've been shafted until you're driving home and the steering wheel comes off in your hands.

I left Inisheer the next day, cycling southwards towards the music of Miltown Malbay, riding the coastline above the Cliffs of Moher, where seventy million waves in seven million years have eaten into seven hundred feet of shale and sandstone, and sheered the land from beneath your feet. It is beautiful; it is cherished for its beauty. But to get there, you must first run through a gauntlet of gaucheness – the taped muzak of "Visions of Ireland," touted as "Ireland's Best-Selling Cassette"; buskers dressed up as leprachauns; ghetto blasters on car rooftops, playing the songs of THE FABULOUS FAMOUS MULROONEY SISTERS, schmalz for sale, the ridiculous before the sublime.

The Mulrooneys are only fabulous in the sense that their music passes the limits of belief, and they are only famous here in this car park; they may, however, be sisters. But they bring back memories of something so excruciatingly embarrassing, so acutely uncomfortable, that it had been banished from thought, submerged into the subconscious. The place: Quebec City. The year: 1985. The event: the so-called Shamrock Summit, when the prime minister of Canada met the president of the United States. The president, it may be recalled, was a man by the name of Reagan, who spent most of his time thinking he was somewhere else. The prime minister, eager to please and desperate to impress, got up on stage with the president, put his arm around him and began singing "When Irish Eyes Are Smiling." The president, lost without his teleprompter, had some difficulty remembering the words and tried hard not to look confused; unfortunately, his considerable acting skills were not quite up to the mark. Oblivious, the prime minister sang on, a saccharine voice before a saccharine orchestra, relishing every moment. Suddenly, in a shock of recognition, the prime minister's name came back to me. It was Mulroney, Brian Mulroney. Could he have been, I wondered, the Missing Brother?

I kept cycling southwards, faster than before, following the folding hills that rose and fell with the coast. The road wove its way around the remains of the West Clare railway, which had once been the principal line of communication in the district. The railway had done fairly well for itself in its time, despite having a schedule that bore only a coincidental resemblance to the actual arrival and departure of its trains. Then, on a fateful day in 1924, a troubadour by the name of Percy French travelled on the line, in the naïve belief that the train would arrive within at least three hours of the stated time. It didn't. He missed his performance, he missed his Guinness, and he missed his bed for the night. So he decided to get even in the traditional bardic manner – by writing a song about the experience, a mock epic called "Are You Right There, Michael, Are You Right?" that described in loving detail how the stoker and the driver would gather twigs and wait for the turf to dry, so they could get enough fuel to make it for another mile down the track.

Shortly after the song was written, the line went bankrupt. And here it stands today, rusting and rotting away, a silent but eloquent testimony to the sheer power of satire in Irish society.

The church spire of Miltown Malbay came in sight, and I began to brace myself for the music festival to end all music festivals, the Willie Clancy Summer School. Willie Clancy was one of Ireland's greatest uilleann pipers; for years now, his home town has celebrated his memory, and musicians from all over the world gather here for the sessions and the lessons, Willie Week, the wildest week of the year. I checked into Leagard House, John and Suzanne Hannon's bed-and-breakfast, a place where you couldn't turn around without bumping into a musician or a story-teller, and settled in for the week.

The first session I went to was at Queally's Pub, just around the corner. A handful of musicians sat by the window, tuning and talking and ordering up their inspiration from the bar. James Kelly, fiddle player, was among them; he started to lilt a reel with his voice, in a kind of Celtic scat singing, while the others smiled their appreciation. Then, suddenly, they broke into the "Tarbolton Reel," playing at a steady, sane pace measured by the tapping of feet on the floor. The accordion player slid straight into a second reel, and the rest followed, without missing a beat; there were high-pitched hoots and whoops of appreciation and encouragement from the crowd.

Students of ethnomusicology have spent many happy hours studying the origin, development, and consolidation of the evolutionary idea of whooping along with sessions, placing particular emphasis on discernable patterns of timing. The general consensus is that the hoots should properly occur under any one of the following three circumstances: a) when there is a lively transition from one tune to another; b) when one of the players produces a particularly impressive roll or ornamentation; and c) when the volume of the session is increased by the addition of one or more new instruments. In my experience, people just do it whenever they feel like doing it.

Towards the end of the second reel, the accordion player shouted out a new key to let the other musicians know where he was going; once again, they all changed gear together, as if they'd been doing it all their lives. When the accordionist had finished, the concertina player took over with a new round of reels; then one of the fiddlers threw out sparks of tunes until one caught fire, and they were all away again.

"You're very quiet," James Kelly told the people who were now cramming themselves into the room. Everyone was focused on the music; without quite realizing it, we were turning the session into a mini-concert. The musicians, picking up the cue, began to act the part of performers, and took it in turns to play solo pieces and slow airs along with the red-hot reels. Among other things, this enabled us to hear the concertina player, whose music had been partially hidden behind the accordion. The concertina was brought into Ireland by proselytizing Salvation Army members towards the end of the last century; for some reason, it became particularly popular in Clare, where it was quickly and easily assimilated into the world of traditional music. Something similar occurred across the Atlantic in colonial America, when British regimental bands brought in their fifes and drums, and black slaves started to play their own kind of music on the instruments, in a style that anticipated jazz. At any rate, the concertina player gave us a tune of his own, before rocketing the session into "The Dublin Reel" and "The Wise Maid," while the ethnomusicologists took notes and the others hooted and hollered to their hearts' content.

A pattern quickly imposed itself on the cheerful anarchy of Willie Week. The day started with music classes at the local school, where you could take lessons in singing, dancing, or any of the instruments commonly associated with traditional music; the only prerequisite was a passable level of competence in the instrument of your choice. At lunchtime, everyone crowded into fast food joints and filled up with fuel for the afternoon sessions that went on throughout the length and breadth of the town. And in the evenings, there was a mini-exodus to the outlying areas, where the pubs were less packed and stayed open longer. Then it was back to the bed-and-breakfast as the stars faded, four or five hours of sleep, and more of the same the next day. Once you started, you couldn't stop until the last musician had played the last reel; the whiplash would have killed you.

The music lessons began at ten o'clock; I signed up for Tin Whistle: Intermediate. There were about a dozen of us in the classroom, in varying stages of sleep-deprived dishevelment. Our instructor looked the worse for wear on the first morning, and progressively deteriorated as the week went on. He never did introduce himself, but in the sessions his mates referred to him as Maggots, for reasons that I feared to guess. Maggots was a brilliant flute and whistle player, but a less than inspiring teacher. He would come in roughly on time, bleary with bloodshot eyes, clinging to a roll-your-own cigarette like a life-belt, and would write the notes of a tune on the blackboard. Then he'd play it through at normal speed, break it into its constituent parts, and get us to follow along. It sounded like pigs in a slaughter house – twelve of us, shrieking out discordant notes that bounced off the concrete walls and reverberated through the hollows of our hang-overs. Maggots would shake his head, draw on his cig, and ask each of us to play the piece separately, thus exposing even more starkly our different degrees of incompetence. By the third morning, I was seriously considering giving up the instrument altogether and settling for the kazoo instead.

From Maggots's point of view, traditional music was not something that could be "taught," and certainly not taught in the space of a week. All you could do, then, was to introduce people to tunes they hadn't heard before, and leave the rest to them. That was why his answers to specific questions were so vague. When he was asked about ornamentations, he did not go into a discussion about the techniques of the cut and the roll and the crann; instead, he just said it was a personal thing, and we should do whatever we felt like doing whenever we wanted. Or again, when one player asked for advice about improving his style, Maggots simply told him that he should "give it more guts," on the grounds that the dance music only worked if it was played with total commitment. In effect, he was teaching us what he knew – that the only real way to learn the music was by listening to it, by getting inside its spirit.

With the lesson over, and our ears ringing with the echoes of high notes hitting hard walls, we would spill out into the schoolyard and begin the Search for the Perfect Session. You never found it, of course. One of the Laws of Festivals is that someone else always stumbles across the session of the century, and always takes sadistic pride in telling you what you missed – if only you'd been here yesterday, if only you'd come with us last night, if only, if only. Still, you did your best. The simplest method was to follow the first fiddle case you saw on the street and see where it led. If you recognized any of the best-known players, you could shadow them at a safe distance and hope they weren't simply looking for the nearest toilet. But basically, you just went from pub to pub, sticking your head in the door, sizing up the situation, and taking it from there.

It was this approach that led me to the back room of Cleary's pub, which became a kind of second home by the middle of the week. Each day, the wind blew different players into the pub, and the music changed with the weather. One afternoon, the place was packed with fiddle players; their music was wild, rambunctious, and intense, a bit like a Scottish Fiddle Orchestra on speed. The next day, two flute players faced off against each other in a high-speed, high-intensity duel, soaring to heights that neither one could have reached alone, against a background of pipes, whistles, fiddles, harps, guitars, bones, and bodhráns. On another occasion, the music was angry and aggressive, led by a banjo player who hit the strings with hatred; he was a guard, or policeman, from Dublin, and he was not the sort of person you would want to be arresting you.

When the afternoon sessions had run their course, it was back to Leagard House for dinner, cold water on the face, and away for the night. Getting to the outlying sessions was easy enough; you just stood by the road, stuck out your thumb, and went wherever your driver happened to be going. On my first night, I wound up at Gleeson's pub in Coor, somewhere to the east, where there was fiddle music and dancing. The musicians must have averaged around a hundred years apiece; the youngest was Junior Crehan, and he couldn't have been much under ninety. They never smiled. In fact, they never even moved; they were known locally as the "Stiff Six." But they knew what they were doing on the fiddles; they played at a significantly slower speed than the youngbloods back in Miltown, and let the music speak through the spaces.

For the rest of the week, my hitch-hiking took me to the village of Mullagh, a street with four pubs, some seven or eight miles southeast of Miltown. There was a kind of late-night Alternative Festival here, stretching long past closing time and breaking up somewhere around dawn. Early in the evenings, you could catch some sean-nós, or old-style, traditional Irish singing. "How can you tell when a sean-nós singer is outside your door?" someone once asked. "He can't find the right key and doesn't know when to come in." In some respects, sean-nós singing is a world unto itself; it adopts the same kind of embellishment and variation that characterizes the dance music, but each song is personal to the point at which it defies musical accompaniment. Not only that, but it's very much an acquired taste, and it's particularly hard on ears accustomed to the smooth sound of your average Irish tenor.

"The mode of reciting ballads in this island is singularly harsh," wrote John Millington Synge when he heard sean-nós singing on a visit to Inisheer back in 1902. "I fell in with a curious man today beyond the east village, and we wandered out on the rocks towards the sea ... He asked me if I was fond of songs, and began singing to show me what he could do. The music was much like what I have heard before on the islands – a monotonous chant with pauses on the high and low notes to mark the rhythm; but the harsh nasal tone in which he sang was almost intolerable. His performance reminded me in general effect of a chant I once heard from a party of Orientals I was travelling with in a third-class carriage from Paris to Dieppe, but the islander ran his voice over a much wider range." Some music scholars have argued that there are close connections between the sean-nós songs of Ireland, with their slides through the scale and their styles of ornamentation, and the ragas of northern India. Others, not to be outdone, maintain that there are links between traditional Irish singing and the music of the Bedouins. Normally, I'd be sceptical; but after listening to the songs in a place like Mullagh, I wouldn't rule anything out.

If Synge was right about the "harsh nasal tone," his description of the Inisheer singer as "a curious man" also strikes a chord. In coffee houses and folk clubs throughout the world, there is a certain type of person, a certain style, that is inextricably associated with the singing tradition. Picture a large, bearded man with a voluminous gut extending beneath an aran sweater; he stands before you with a pint of beer in one hand, and the index finger of the other lodged firmly in his ear. He leans his head back, closes his eyes, tightens his nostrils, and forces a long, drawn-out sound that eventually slides into something approaching song: "Nnnnnyyyyyaaaaa-as I roved out on a bright May morning." And he simply will not stop.

You're up to verse thirty-four now, and it slowly dawns on you that he's not even half way through; all the people around you are looking at their feet, and you don't know whether it's because they're engrossed in the song or because they're praying that it will soon be over. Finally, mercifully, it draws to a close, and you find yourself simultaneously sighing with relief and applauding along with everyone else. If anyone calls for an encore, though, your sideways glance would probably slice him in two.

But in Mullagh, the stereotype was shattered. Here, I was listening to the real thing, rather than folkie imitations. In the sparse surroundings of a village pub, an old man sang a ballad about a shipwreck, his voice taut and tense and tuneful, expressing emotions through compressing them, weaving the song around its own variations, and drawing out a sense of anguish and loss that seemed to speak for an entire way of life. As he sang, a friend held his wrist and turned it in slow, rhythmic circles, in a communion of the spirit.

There wasn't only sean-nós singing in Mullagh; you could also hear a wide variety of eighteenth- and nineteenth-century songs from across the British Isles. These songs took you into the world that lay beneath the "official" culture, a world peopled by highwaymen, cross-dressers, and deceitful lovers. The highwaymen were usually social bandits, people who rebelled against unjust laws or cruel masters, and went on the run to retain their liberty; they'd sleep in ditches by day and travel the roads by night, preying on the landlords and protected by the people. In songs like "Allan Tyne of Harrow," the hero would pioneer a modest redistribution-of-wealth program that reached back to Robin Hood and looked forward to the welfare state:

One night I robbed at Turnham Green, a revenue collector,
And what I got I gave it to a widow to protect her.
I always robbed the rich and great, to rob the poor I scorn it
And now in iron chains I'm bound, in doom I do lie borned.

They were usually betrayed in the end, hanged in public spectacles where the authorities paraded their power in a style that was open and theatrical. Many of the broadsheet ballads contained the "last words" or the "dying confession" of the condemned man – words that were usually made up well in advance by streetmongers who would hawk the songs for a small profit.

Then there were the cross-dressing songs, which usually unfolded in the following sequence: Two lovers, generally known as "Willie" and "Nancy," are about to get married, when the dreaded press gang arrives and unceremoniously carts Willie off to sea. Nancy, not to be deterred, decides to follow him. So she dresses herself up as a sailor or a cabin-boy, smears her fingers with a touch of tar, signs on board, and starts to look for her Willie. Meanwhile, the captain, much to his surprise, finds that he has strange feelings of affection towards this new cabin-boy, and begins to experience a crisis of sexual identity. All is revealed, though, when there is a skirmish on the ship, the buttons fly off her jacket, and her snow-white breast appears for all to see. The captain breathes a large sigh of relief.

But where is Willie? At this stage, it becomes apparent that perhaps Willie wasn't really worth following after all; you might even conclude that he had arranged the press gang himself to escape the marriage. In some versions, the captain tells Nancy to get up early the next morning, when she'll find Willie walking along with his "lady gay," whom he just happened to have married the previous day. In others, Willie finds out that she's after him and is really pissed off. So much so, in fact, that he and his mates plan to do her in:

> We'll tie her hands behind her back and overboard she'll go,
> We'll tie her hands behind her back, she'll die a public show.

But Nancy is not the kind of woman you'd want to mess around with. According to one variation on the theme, she takes out a brace of pistols and promptly dispatches Willie to an early grave; according to others, the captain steps in and threatens to throw Willie overboard. Either way, she comes out pretty well of the situation. At the very least, she is rewarded with her own vessel, sailing out to the Isle of Man; at the very best, she winds up living as "the highest captain's wife, in Canadee-i-o."

The cross-dressing woman is nothing if not resourceful; instead of lamenting cruel fate, she goes out and makes things happen. Nor is she entirely fictional; every so often, eighteenth-century historians stumble across reports and records of real women who passed for men and joined the navy. But the predominant image of women in the song tradition is that of the passive, pining, and ultimately faithful female, the woman who stands by her man. This appears most clearly in the "broken token" genre of songs, which begin – inevitably, one comes to feel – with the singer roving out on a bright May morning and encountering a woman in the throes of "sad lamentation," as opposed to "happy lamentation." The protagonist boldly approaches her and asks her what's wrong. Man trouble, of course; her lover has been fighting for King and Country, the wars are over, and he hasn't come home. What's his name, asks the newcomer. Willie, comes the reply; he might have known. Wait a minute, says the man; I knew Willie very well. We were best of friends, in fact. At this point, she should smell a rat. But she doesn't.

Depending on the particular song, the stranger will try any one of a number of lines here. Willie is a false young man; you'd be better off forgetting him and coming along with me. Or: Willie's ship sank off the coast of Spain and he was drowned; you'd be better off forgetting him and coming along with me. Or, even less tactfully: Willie was slain by a French soldier while fighting the "bold Napoleon Boney" on the plains of Waterloo, and gasping "fare thee well my lovely Nancy" with his last breath; you'd be better off forgetting him and coming along with me. She falls into a swoon, and swears that

If Willie is drownded, no man on earth I'll take
But through lonesome glens and valleys, I'll wander for his sake.

In the true folk fashion, her rosy cheeks turn "to pale and to wan." Nobody is sure exactly what that means, but the general complexion is not good.

And then, suddenly and dramatically, the stranger reveals his True Identity: "Nancy, I'm the Man!" Faint not, gentle reader; it is none other than Willie himself. To prove it, he takes out a ring that they broke between them as a token of their love, and as a means of mutual recognition in the seemingly improbable event that each one should forget what the other looked like.

Now, you might think that this relationship spelled trouble. After all, Willie has put Nancy through emotional hell, has tried to seduce her in the guise of a stranger, and has put her loyalty to the test. Nancy, for her part, couldn't even remember what her darling Willie looked like. You might think that they'd have one Holy Row and never speak to each other again. But you'd be wrong. This was 1815; Nancy stopped wandering around the woods in a swoon, fell into Willie's arms, passed the test, married her man, and did the dishes for the rest of her life.

Every so often, though, the story line takes an unexpected twist. In one song, "Sovay, Sovay," the protagonist is rolling along happily in a coach-and-six, chatting away to his fellow passengers, when a masked highwayman rides down from the hills and robs the lot of them. After lightening everyone's pockets, the highwayman points a pistol at our hero's breast and demands that he hand over the gold ring on his finger. No way, comes the reply; that's the ring my true love gave me; you'll have to shoot me before I'll give it up – at which point the highwayman wheels around on his horse and rides off into the sunset, sans ring. Now fast forward to the following day. Our hero is in the garden with his true love, when he notices that she has suddenly acquired a large collection of gold watches that are suspiciously similar to those worn by the passengers on the coach. As one might expect, he makes some tentative inquiries about just how they came into her possession. So she tells all – how she dressed herself up in men's attire, put on a highwayman's mask, bought a pistol, and decided to see just how much he loved her. This one has everything – a highwayman, cross-dressing, and the loyalty test. It's just as well that he passed:

> Had you handed me the ring, she said,
> I'd have pulled the trigger, pulled the trigger,
> And shot you dead.

And so it ends; presumably, they lived dysfunctionally ever after.

The singing generally went on to around midnight, when the pubs closed in Miltown and the overspill flooded into Mullagh. Carload after carload came in, crammed to capacity; if it was possible to squeeze eight musicians into a mini, then eight musicians would be squeezed into a mini. It was; they were. The sessions became almost as packed themselves, and stayed that way until they were eventually broken up by the late-night forays of the guards. Sometime between three and seven in the morning, a police car would park ostentatiously on the street, just to let the publicans know that they'd better start clearing out their premises. The publicans, equally ostentiously, would order everyone out, and make sure they were seen to be leaving, just to let the guards know that their message had been received and understood. Then the guards would drive away, the doors would reopen, the diehards would return, and the session would resume, safely sealed off in a back room.

But on the last night of the festival, the guards broke the rules; they came back. We were all in the back kitchen, playing up a storm, when we heard a slow, insistent, irregular thumping beneath the music. Our first instinct was to look for the delinquent bodhrán player; but before we could so much as turn around, the door had been forced open and two very large guards were towering over us. "You'll all get out, and get out now!" barked the Senior Officer like an Angry God. "Give us a song," shouted one of the less intimidated and more intoxicated fiddle players. "I'll give you a song all right," he said. "It's called 'Your Day in Court,' and you'll be singing it soon enough if you don't clear out." "Ah, c'mon, just one more set of tunes to finish the night," came the cry; we turned into little kids trying to squeeze an extra few minutes before bedtime. "One more, and that's it. After that, I'll book the lot of you."

And, like little kids, we exploited his concession to the utmost. The last set seemed to stretch into eternity; a wild, intense, frenetic energy took over, as if this was the last night in the world, and these were our last breaths of music and life. But when the guards returned, as return they did, there was no choice; the landlady's licence was hanging by a thread, and we had to get out in short order. "Out the back way," she shouted. "And don't make a sound."

Out the back way. A ragged band of blind-drunk musicians, fumbling and groping in the dark, bumping into walls, falling into ditches, lost for everything except words. This way, over here; no, this way, through the hedge; can't see a thing; christ, I've banged me nose; shut up, the guards'll hear you; follow me over this wall; jesus, I can see your knickers; shut your eyes and shut your mouth; which way now; how the hell should I know – oh, christ, it's the guards. "Hello, lads, it's a grand night to be out for a stroll in the shite, is it not?" "We're just on our way home, now." "It's just as well for you that you are. Drive safely." "We will, we will." And so, it was back to Miltown, with the first glimmer of dawn appearing in the eastern sky.

At the end of Willie Week, my system was in a state of shock; I decided to stay at Leagard House a little longer and just stare out to sea until the mist cleared and the body became reconnected with the mind. Gradually, the guests left, except for a handful of hard-core musicians who refused to believe that it was over; they congregated at the Central Hotel and played one last session for posterity. Among them was an English woman who'd first visited Ireland the previous summer, stumbled across Miltown by chance, and become an instant convert. By the time she got home, she'd decided to give up her job, buy a fiddle, play six hours a day, and live for her music. I'd felt the same impulse myself. The sessions are addictive; they draw you into their warmth, they enfold you and exhilarate you, they get into your bloodstream until all that matters is your next fix of music. You can find yourself, but you can also lose yourself, as well.

By the next day, the last musician had played the last reel. Miltown, where the streets had been packed with people and the pubs had been bursting with life, seemed like a shell of itself, a ghost town, where empty chip-bags blew across half-deserted roads. A handful of old men talked together in a shop doorway; a group of kids hung around on the corner, waiting for something to do. All the air had gone out of the tyre.

The Gold Ring

"The Gold Ring" – there's a story attached to that name. A long, long time ago – if I were there then, I wouldn't be there now; if I were there then and now, I would have a new story or an old story, or I might have no story at all – the birds could talk, giants roamed the land, and fairy music filled the air. There was a farmer, and he was walking across the fields one night, when he heard the faint strains of music in the distance. Moving closer, he saw a fairy piper playing a fairy dance. But when the fairies sensed his presence, they scattered into the woods and vanished into the earth. The farmer went up to the place where the piper had played and there he found a tiny gold ring lying on the ground. So he put it in his pocket, carried it home, and took out his fiddle to celebrate his good fortune with a few reels. But when he put the bow across the strings, he couldn't get a decent sound of it at all, save for the scratching of an old key in an old lock. And no matter how much he played that fiddle, not a note could he get out of it.

So, the next night, he returned with the ring and his fiddle to the place where he had found the fairies, and he waited and he waited. And just as the first glimmer of dawn appeared over the eastern sky, he heard the faint rustle of soft feet on golden leaves. When he turned around, he came face to face with the fairy piper.

"I've come for what is mine," says the piper. "For if truth be told, I can't play a slide or a jig or a reel without that ring." "You can have it and welcome," said the farmer. "For if truth be told, I can't play a slide or a jig or a reel with it." And he tossed the ring back, and took out his fiddle, and played the finest reel of his life. And the fairy piper picks up the ring, and takes out his pipes, and plays the finest jig that human ears had ever heard. "Would you ever be after teaching me that tune?" asked the farmer. "I would so," says the fairy piper, and they sat down together until the farmer had it. "And what would it be called?" asked the farmer. "The Gold Ring," says the fairy piper, disappearing into the half-light of dawn.

I am cycling southwards now, from County Clare towards the Rings of Kerry. The wheels turn me from Kilrush to Killimer, down to the Shannon, where black waves of rain sweep over the river, and where the ferry coughs its way across to Kerry. Chills of water trickle down neck and back, as I speed towards the turf fires and hot toddies of the town of Listowel.

Listowel is this year's site of the Fleadh Cheoil, the Orgy of Music, organized by Comhaltas Ceoltóirí Éireann, the traditional music, song, and dance society of Ireland. The Comhaltas members are the Keepers of the Tradition, and they approach their task with a single-mindedness that is awe-inspiring in its intensity. During the Fleadh, they organize competitions in the school, so that they can check the musical pulse of the nation. In each category – fiddle, pipes, flute, whistle, and so on – the competitors take turns playing the same piece in front of a panel of judges. The musicians look like frightened rabbits caught in the headlights; the judges look like the ones driving the car. Skills are displayed and sentences are pronounced. It is all so antiseptic.

"Comhaltas Interruptus," someone said with a snort. This music belongs in pubs and kitchens, not schoolrooms and competitions. It thrives on spontaneity, devilment, and irreverence; regimentation and green-jacketed respectability only stifle it. Listowel has 5000 people and fifty-eight pubs, and it's here that you'll find the heart of the music: in Lynch's Bar, where three Mayo men play for seven hours without stopping; the Horseshoe, where a German group called Limerick Junction rush through the reels, more Irish than the Irish; Sheahan's pub and grocery shop, where a battery of uilleann pipers from Derry belts out the music like a bothy band of old.

Or go down to the Listowel Arms in the centre of town. In the foyer, two brilliant musicians from the Shetland Islands are surrounded by a spellbound crowd. The fiddler plays in the dark, sparse tones of Donegal, Scotland, and Cape Breton; the guitarist provides a jazz accompaniment in the style of Django Reinhardt, and the mixture is explosive. Most people are going wild over it, but the begrudgers are about. "They're murdering our music, murderin' it," mutters the man next to me, shaking his head in horror. "This is not how it's supposed to be played." And I could imagine him prowling through the sessions with a blackthorn stick, ready to rap the knuckles of anyone who deviated from the True Faith by introducing heretical instruments like the guitar and playing heretical chords like flattened sevenths or diminished ninths. He'd flatten and diminish you, all right, all in the name of purity and tradition.

And then, when the Fleadh is over and you're Irished out, you can sleep for sixteen hours and drive back home with your mates, stopping at every second pub on the way. One of the Derry lads told me later about his journey back to the North. By the middle of the afternoon, he wanted a break from traditional music, to enjoy the silence, and he asked the driver to turn the cassette player off for a while. "What are you talking about?" came the reply; "we don't even have a radio in this car." Sleep-deprived, alcohol-induced audio-hallucinations of non-stop session music – now that, he said, was a sure sign of a good Fleadh.

Leaving Listowel on the bicycle, "The Gold Ring" in my ear, I travelled on past Tralee and raced the cloud-line towards the Dingle Peninsula, the first of the Rings of Kerry. The Slieve Mish mountains stretch like a spine down to Dunquin; then they break into the Blasket Islands, disappear into the Atlantic, and are born again three thousand miles later in Newfoundland and Nova Scotia. I cycled past Kilvar Strand, a golden torc around the neck of the sea, and began the seemingly endless climb up the Conor Pass, slow spirals on a clear day. The energy fell and the spirits rose with every turn of the pedals; at the top, the southwestern world was spread beneath my feet – Loop Head peering down from County Clare in the north, the dark mountains of the Ivereagh Peninsula to the south, the ancient monasteries of the Skellig Rocks far out in the Atlantic. And then the road dropped straight down to Dingle itself, directly below and coming up fast.

Dingle has flourished with the tourist boom; there are hotels and restaurants and bed-and-breakfasts, and houses with the smell of fresh paint. The pubs are full of tourist-driven traditional music, but the best sessions happen at the Hillgrove Hotel, where the dancing begins around midnight. The music is provided by Seamas Begley, a brilliant accordionist from down the road, and Steve Cooney, a brilliant guitarist from down under, that otherworld they call Australia. Somewhere in his travels, he learned to play in the flamenco style, and applies it to Irish dance music with dazzling effect. He's also been known to play jigs and reels on the didgery-doo, but that's another story.

The dancing is as wild as the mountains – an exuberance of legs, kicking high in the air, kaleidoscopes across the floor, a syncopation of shouts and steps. This is what it must have been like in the old days, before the priests got hold of it and took all the sex out. What passes for traditional dancing in much of Ireland today is very much a modern invention; it combines the fakery of nineteenth-century Celtic costumes with the rigidity of Irish Catholic Victorian morality, and it's about as spontaneous as a politician's speech. Any sign of movement in the pelvic area would bring down an army of avenging angels, threatening you with hellfire and damnation, and making sure that you get back on the straight and narrow.

But in a few pockets of Irish culture, the original tradition has survived. You can still see it in Newfoundland, where the Irish who emigrated in the eighteenth century and lived in the remote outports were able to escape the attention of bowdlerizing priests. Their dancing is full of fancy footwork and pelvic thrusts, like Mick Jagger doing the jig. And so it is with the set-dancers of Dingle, as they weave and spin with the spirit of the music. There was nothing remotely wholesome about it at all; it was wonderful.

The next day took me around the peninsula on the Slea Head road, where the coastline has been clawed upwards by a giant's fingers, shipwrecks scatter the shore, and clouds curl around Eagle Mountain. The Blaskets come into view, the islands where story-tellers once upon a time enchanted spirits from the fire, and where heaven lay a foot and a half above the height of a man. And back again to the southeast, there are beehive huts of stone that shel-tered the people of the peninsula from the wind of centuries. I got off the bike and walked towards them through a stone-filled farmer's field where the goats were grazing. An old woman with a black shawl came down from the cottage; she wished me a good day, chatted for half an hour about the weather, and casually suggested that perhaps a pound would be a fair price to charge people for seeing the huts. It would indeed, I said, taking the money out of my pocket and walking inside the walls, which still shield you from the elements. As I was leaving, I could hear a child's voice: "Did that man give you money to look at the goats, gramma?" "Don't be a fool," she told him. "'Twas to look at the stones."

At the end of the day, I booked into a bed-and-breakfast, rewarded myself with a pint at the village pub, and then watched the TV weather forecast with considerable consternation. Normally, you could happily ignore everything the forecasters said; like econ-omists, they made predictions not because they knew, but because they were asked. In any case, they liked to keep all their options open by covering the map of Ireland with smiling suns, white clouds, black clouds, clouds that had rain coming out of them, clouds that had no rain coming out of them, clouds that blocked the sun, clouds that didn't block the sun, arrows of wind that pointed in all directions at once, arrows that presented you with every imaginable windspeed. Not today, though. Superimposed on the entire map of Ireland were three ominous words: DANGER OF

FLOODING. The downpour would hit the southwest at ten the next morning, they said. For once, they were right.

I was in Cahirciveen on the Ivereagh Peninsula, the second ring, when it struck. I'd set off at six in the morning, the first time on my trip that I'd seen the dawn when sober. The storm clouds were gathering over McGillycuddy's Reeks, carrying the first drops of rain on a light wind. And then the wind became stronger and the rain became thicker and the sky became blacker, until wind and rain and sky were one, howling over hills and houses, drenching the western world. Rivers sprang to life on hillsides, cascading water across narrow roads; drains spilled over pavements; gutters overflowed; sheets of wetness washed over empty streets. I knew there were mountains here because I'd seen them from the Conor Pass; all I could see today, though, were clouds of water rolling like waves over the land. Pedals turned slowly and sluggishly against the wind, while the storm shrieked through the streets of Waterville and the palm trees bent double in its path. And then the long climb into the mountains, as high as the herons, before a hairpin bend suddenly released me from the pressure and sent me flying with the wind. Flying past Derrynane, Dan O'Connell country; flying past Knocknagullion, past the Ballaghbeama Gap, and into Kenmare, for recovery and rest and warmth.

Five weeks and five days later, the storm subsided and the world became dry again. I made a mental note to myself: Next time, be sure to bring rain gear. And from Kenmare, I set off on the third of the Rings of Kerry, the Beare Peninsula, the remotest ring of all. You pass through a tunnel of green, enfolded by hedges and arching trees, and emerge into a soft, dark wilderness of waterfalls and mountains. At the village of Urhan, I decided to leave the road and follow a path across the hills to Allihies; it became steeper and steeper, and then petered out into rocks and rubble, more suitable for mountain goats than mountain bikes. But the views were spectacular, with the main road switchbacking around Cod's Head, and the Kenmare River flowing into the sea past Dursey Island, to which you can cross in a rust-covered, creaking cable car that looks as though it hasn't been serviced since the early Iron Age.

I stopped that night in Glengariff, tucked into the northeast corner of Bantry Bay, before heading south to the island of Cape Clear, on the southwestern edge of Ireland. I took the boat from Baltimore, bicycle on board, on a rare summer's day. This was a world away from Whitehead and Islandmagee, Gaelic speakers on a wild tract of land, windswept hills before the Atlantic, Fastnet Rock in the far south. I sat by the cliffs, played songs for the seagulls, and slept under the sun; the weariness of seven hundred miles and seven hundred pints and seven hundred worries lifted itself into the sky and blew away like an autumn leaf on a westering breeze.

But the evening found me back in Baltimore, minding my own business in the corner of a pub. Two singers came in, set up the microphones, tuned their guitars, and clicked into their automatic-pilot Irish entertainment routine – "Kilgarry Mountain," "Jug of Punch," the usual suspects. As the place filled up, the calls went out for a few good rebel songs, songs that would stir your blood. And if rebel songs were what we wanted, then rebel songs were what we'd have – "Four Green Fields," "Kevin Barry," "A Nation Once Again." And when the evening ended, everyone stood up for the Southern National Anthem, "The Soldier's Song":

> We'll sing a song, a soldier's song,
> With cheering, rousing chorus
> As round our blazing fires we throng,
> The starry heavens o'er us
> Impatient for the coming fight,
> And as we wait the morning's light,
> Here in the silence of the night
> We'll chant a soldier's song.

Always the coming fight, always the romantic chorus before the squalid death. The weight of weariness began to press down on me again; for some reason, I hadn't expected to encounter the old romantic nationalist fervour here, in a holiday pub, after such a day of peace. I felt heavy, too heavy to get to my feet. Suddenly, the lads next to me yanked me up by my shoulders, so I could pay the proper respect to the nation. I mean, this is our National Anthem, and people here should respect it. And if you don't respect it, you should take yourself somewhere else. I mean, if we were living in your country, we would respect your anthem. So we'd expect you to respect ours. All right?

Perhaps this place wasn't so far away from Whitehead and Island-magee after all.

The Boy in the Gap

I travelled from Cork to Dublin in an alcoholic fog,
remembering nothing.

The Wheels of the World

You notice the fumes first, belching out from the exhaust pipes of a million buses that are painted like a bad joke in the green colours of an Irish spring; clouds of carbon monoxide choke the air, sting the eyes, and sour the mouth. Next, you see shards of glass strewn along the kerbside, just waiting to tear your tyres to shreds. But it is dangerous to look downwards for too long, for you must keep your eyes on the anarchy of cars and lorries coming at you like a speeded-up video game. And you'd better notice them, because they sure won't notice you; cyclists, becoming invisible the instant they turn the pedals, are cut off, squeezed out, and knocked down. If you get too close to the line of parked cars, you will become a victim of the Let's-Open-the-Car-Door-without-Looking trick and be splattered like a bird flying into a window. But if you go more than a door's-length away from the line of parked cars, you will either be run over from behind without warning, or sideswiped from either direction without warning. And if you're really unlucky, you might be car-doored, hit from behind, and sideswiped all at once, while choking from poisonous gas and having your tyres ripped apart by broken bottles.

In short, Dublin is a cyclist's nightmare, to be avoided at all costs.

The pubs are about as crowded as the roads, and the drinking matches the intensity of the driving. Finding a good traditional music pub appears easy, but actually turns out to be quite a challenge; you'll be directed to places like The Blarney Stone or Kitty O'Shea's, places so packed that you can hardly breathe, places so loud that not even an army of accordions could make themselves heard. The microphones give it away; you'll get lots of rowdy-dowdy stuff and plenty of performances, but you'll be looking long and hard for the decent sessions.

They do exist, though; you can hear some fine music most evenings at Hughes's pub on Chancery Lane, or on a Sunday afternoon at Slattery's on Capel Street. The standard of playing is better at Hughes's, but the atmosphere is friendlier at Slattery's. Anywhere between a dozen and a score of musicians group themselves round a raft of tables, and bring out their banjos and mandolins and guitars and bodhráns and fiddles and flutes and whistles. If you get there early enough, you can usually find a seat close to the players; if not, you can always rub shoulders with the people standing strategically between the banjos and the bar, and talk and drink and listen until they throw you out for Holy Hour.

I am there with a friend and her three-year-old son, who is bouncing up and down to the music through a forest of grown-up legs. Someone hoists him up so that he can see the musicians, and points out the different instruments to him. One of the bodhrán players lets him bang on the drum for a while; a whistle player lends

him her whistle, which he blows with much enthusiasm in a shrill monotone of happiness. He watches the fiddle players with fascination, as the pints are passed over his head and the laughter rings about his ears. A few days later, when I was lying on the floor with him at home and flicking through the channel-changer, the National Symphony Orchestra suddenly appeared on the screen. He stood up, transfixed, and took in the scene – bow-ties, long dresses, violins, piccolos. "Daybid," he said, in brow-furrowed bewilderment, "that's a funny kind of a pub."

I will not stay in Dublin long; the air is too thick, the streets too crowded. Instead, I will link up with one of the great cycling events of the year, the annual Dublin–Belfast Maracycle, and head back across the border. The Maracycle is put on by Cooperation North, an organization that tries to foster north-south understanding by bringing people together and breaking some of the barriers. A thousand or so cyclists from the North travel down the hundred miles from Belfast to Dublin, where they are wined and dined until they drop. Then, the next day, they're joined by a couple of thousand southerners on the road to Belfast; after a night of revelry, the Dubliners will summon up whatever strength is left and straggle back home. It's not a race, and it doesn't really matter how long you take, as long as you can complete each leg in a day; apart from that, anything goes.

We assembled at the Royal Dublin Society grounds at seven in the morning – people with spandex suits and state-of-the-art bicycles, people with faded denims and old clunkers, boneshakers and penny-farthings, young bucks on speedsters, elderly couples on tandems, all readying themselves for the road. There was a rich variety of costumes, a halloween party on wheels; Spiderman was there, along with half a dozen Supermen, who would probably melt inside their outfits by the time they reached Dundalk. There was a World War One pilot, with goggles and flying cap, and makeshift wings strapped to his sides. Next to him was a French waiter, holding a tray with a bottle of champagne and two glasses, which he planned to carry all the way to Belfast; good luck over the Mourne Mountains, called out a sceptical Ulster voice. Tommy Sands, a folksinger from County Down, came along for the ride as well; one of his songs, "I'm Going Back on the Bicycle," was being played over the sound system and set the mood for the morning.

To allow a smooth passage through the city, the start was staggered, and we all left in our own detachments. Northern accents mingled in with the softer sounds of the south, and some of the lads decided to bolster their spirits by singing "The Sash My Father Wore," the classic Orange marching song. It was slightly different from the usual version, though; in a wonderful display of ecumenical sacrilege, they sang it in Gaelic. Eventually, my number was called, and the pedals began to turn slowly northwards. I felt in reasonably good shape and began to gather up speed; before I knew it, I was on the outside lane, moving steadily past the stream of cyclists on my left. Suddenly, I felt a hand on the small of my back, and my speed increased by half as much again; I was being pushed along by a tall fellow on a racing bike. "C'mon," he said, laughing as he let go and sped past me; "if you're going to overtake everyone, you should at least go at a decent speed." Then he disappeared into the distance.

Eventually, you settle into a comfortable rhythm and form groups with other cyclists who are going at the same speed. Normally, cycling is a solitary experience – you, your bike, and the road. But the communalism of the Maracycle is exhilarating; you become part of the group, with everyone offering encouragement to each other. By the time we crossed into Northern Ireland, about twenty of us had formed a close-knit community on wheels, cycling together in a two-line pack. The pair in the front would watch out for pot-holes, shield us from the wind, and set the speed; if they were going too fast, someone at the back would shout for a slightly slower pace, and if they were going too slowly, there'd be calls to pick it up a bit. We formed a kind of chain as we cycled. After about ten minutes, the inside lead cyclist would accelerate and shift to the front of the outside line; the next two cyclists behind him would take over the lead, and everyone in the loop would change position accordingly. This not only meant that the task of providing a slipstream for the others was shared equally; it also meant that you got to cycle next to different people every time the line moved.

And so the conversations changed as the chains turned; by the time we reached Banbridge, it was like having reunions with old friends. If Cooperation North wanted the exchange of ideas and cross-fertilization of cultures, it may have succeeded only too well. The Southerners I spoke to were singularly impressed by the high quality of the Northern roads and by the low price of the Northern Guinness – two not insignificant items if you're riding a bike on a hot day. Many of them seemed well on the way to becoming Unionists. The Northern Protestants, for their part, were wildly enthusiastic about the Dublin nightlife, the carefree atmosphere on the streets, and the warm welcome they'd received. Many of them seemed well on the way to becoming Nationalists.

At ten-mile intervals on the route, the organizers had set up rest-points where you could take a break, replenish your liquid supply, and receive massages for aching muscles. Some of the Northerners, who'd learned a few things on the previous day's trip, would drop out at strategic locations, complaining about terrible twinges in their legs and commenting that the physiotherapist at that particular point had the reputation of being very good with her fingers; that was the last we'd ever see of them. But the rest of us stuck together into Belfast, afraid that if we stopped we'd never be able to start up again, and buoyed up one another's spirits with the occasional song. As we closed in on Belfast, we summoned up unexpected strength and started to race in, until we came up the Malone Road into Queen's University. A wave of euphoria swept over us; a jazz band was playing "Tuxedo Junction," pints of lager were being served, laughter was in the air. Our tightly knit group unravelled into the crowd, back into the threads of separate lives. I celebrated with three fast pints, soaked in the sunshine, and meandered over to an old friend's house. "I'll just have a lie-down for a few minutes before tea," I told him when I arrived. Fourteen hours later, I woke up.

I spent most of the next day sitting quietly around Botanic Avenue cafés, rewarding myself with rhubarb pie and cream, over-dosing on caffeine, gearing up for the city's sessions. People in Belfast go to parties with the same spirit of total commitment and dedication that people in Toronto take to their work; you need to prepare yourself carefully. That night, my friends took me into the Docks, a wasteland of bricked up terraced houses, where a handful of pubs have survived against all the odds. We wound up at Pat's Bar, listening to a group of brilliant musicians who'd taken over the back room, pouring down the pints and belting out the tunes. The fiddle player, not much over nineteen, was one of the best I'd heard on my travels, and the guitarist was setting off chain reactions of rhythmic energy with open-tuning accompaniments. Every so often, someone would start singing – a beautiful, gentle tune like "My Cavan Girl," or a lively, mischievous melody like Andy M. Stewart's "The Rambling Rover," with its celebration of lunatics and life:

> If you're bent with arth-er-itis
> Your bowels have got colitis
> You've gallopin' bollockitis
> And you're thinkin' it's time you died;
> If you've been a man of action
> And you're lyin' there in traction
> You may gain some satisfaction
> Thinkin' 'Jesus at least I tried.'

It may have been written by a Scot, but if anything sums up the spirit of the Belfast session scene, that was it.

The following night found us at another pub in the Docks, the Rotterdam. For obscure and obtuse reasons, Belfast has been rather short on tourists; as a result, the sessions here are closer to the tradition than in a place like Dublin or even Galway. We sat down with an American whom I'd last seen at the Ballyshannon Folk Festival; the world of traditional music is a fairly small one, and it doesn't take long before you start running into familiar faces. A couple of other lads joined us, and joined in the crack. The pub had been robbed the night before, they said; two men had come in wearing balaclavas and touting AK 47s, told everyone to lie on the ground, taken the till and robbed the customers. The lads were puzzled about it, though, because the robbery had taken place early on in the evening, before the place had filled up and the coffers were full. "Probably a training run," said one. "Just practisin' for the real thing," said his mate.

Their nonchalant tone evidently struck the American as surprising. "Does this kind of thing happen a lot around here?" he inquired. Wrong question. Beware of Bull. "Ach, no, not too often, hardly ever at all. Not on a Monday night before eight, that's for sure." "No, that's the kind of thing you'd expect more on Fridays," chipped in his mate. "Aye Fridays are bad, right enough. But you're generally all right in the middle of the week; and it's been a full two weeks since this place was hit on a weeknight." "Ah no, you're wrong there," came a voice from the next table. "I was in here last Tuesday when the boys with the balaclavas came in. They had us all lyin' on the floor, like, gettin' our money off of us. An' one fellow, he had no money on him, an' he was scared shitless, beggin' 'em to take his American Express, so he was. So they took his whole fuckin' wallet, just to make him feel better."

"Jeez," said the American, who had been totally taken in by this tissue of lies, "how can you people live like this?" "Ah, well, it's not all that bad, you know. Sure it's not as bad as it's made out to be." "Not at all; sure you get used to it right enough. It's just a matter of never taking any more money with you than you'd need for the evening's pints." The American shuffled uneasily in his seat: "Jeez, I've got eighty pounds on me." "You're gettin' the next fuckin' round," said the first lad; "you're better off spendin' it on us than on the fuckin' terrorists, know what I mean?" "Eighty quid?" said lad number two; "that's a serious amount of money. Best put it somewhere safe, if you ask me." "Aye, best put it in your shoes," confirmed the voice from the next table; "they'd never look in your shoes." "Forty quid in each," someone else suggested, "just to be on the safe side, like." And they nodded their heads in approval as he slid the notes into his socks, and glanced repeatedly at the door, another innocent victim of Belfast bullshit.

As the musicians started into their sets, the lads began to reminisce about the Good Old Days of the early seventies, when they surfed and turfed on the wave of the Troubles. They'd got it down to a fine art, in those days. They would go out to the most expensive restaurant in town and select the most expensive items on the menu. Then, at a prearranged time, just as they were finishing their last glass of Châteauneuf-du-Pape, their mate back home would phone in with a bombscare: "Yous have all got three minutes to get out, like." The place would instantly empty and the customers would scatter on the streets – leaving the lads scot free, with full stomachs and full pockets.

The situation, as they say, is tragic, but never serious.

Before long, the session was going full swing, with a wonderful combination of flutes and fiddles and pipes. The American, who was now known throughout the bar as Bigfoot, was sent on regular missions to buy rounds of Guinness, as the doors opened to more and more musicians. Desi Wilkinson came in with his flute; Tara and Dermi Diamond, on flute and fiddle, followed close behind; Andy the Englishman joined in the violin section. Ciarán Carson was there, puffing away on the flute, making sure that the session etiquette was in order – that the punters made their yelps of approval in the right places, that the boys with the tape recorders asked for permission first, that the autograph hunters waited until after the set was over before mobbing the musicians and showering them with offers of sex. One of the boys at the bar, who'd done a bit of reading up on it all and knew what was what, bought him a pint in appreciation; Ciarán raised his flute in acknowledgment, and your man twitched his thumb in a textbook response.

Meanwhile, the lads were telling Bigfoot why the sessions were so good in Ireland. "The way I see it," said one, "it's all to do with the fact that there are no jobs here. See

these lads? They couldn't find work if they were paid to. So they sit around at home and play the flute or the fiddle or what-have-you all fuckin' day every fuckin' day of the week, 'cos they've got sweet fuck-all else to do. And of course if you do that, you're bound to get pretty decent after a while, even if you made a bollocks of it all to begin with." "Fair enough," said his mate. "But it's not just the jobs, if you ask me. It's the rain that's behind it all." The rain? "Aye, right enough. I mean, you may have noticed, that it pisses down all the shaggin' time in this god-forsaken hole, so it does. So what else are you going to do but stay inside? And where better to stay inside but a pub? And if you get free pints for playin' a few tunes, well, why not?" We looked at him in silent wonder. "That's just my fuckin' opinion, mind," he added after a long pause.

So much for Tuesday. On Wednesday, my friends took me to a different place, the formidable-sounding Antrim Road Christian Brothers' Past Pupils' Association, where the weekly ceilidh was going on and dancing lessons were being given. My friends felt that the dancing tradition needed to be safeguarded against excessively enthusiastic outsiders like me, who tended to get pissed out of their minds and pogo-dance randomly through the room, while everyone else traced precisely prescribed patterns of intricate footwork across the floor. Besides, there was a shortage of men at the ceilidhs, and any male bodies with a breath of life in them would do. So, they took me through the basic steps, the sevens and the threes, and walked me through the basic dances, the "Haymaker's" and the "Walls of Limerick."

More people filtered into the dance hall, the lessons drew to an end, and the ceilidh proper began. You join hands in a line of four facing four, go through your moves, and then pass on through to the next group. And as you meet each new group, you encounter a wide range of responses. One line of dancers might be impatient with or hostile towards beginners, annoyed that they screw things up and disrupt the established order; the next might be encouraging and sympathetic and friendly, eager to show you how it works. There are people who never smile, people who fall over themselves with laughter, people who dance with corks up their asses, and people who weave freely about the floor. Some of the women will hold you at a distance, with tensed-up bodies and wire-taut arms; others will cuddle up close and enjoy the contact. A ceilidh dance is a microcosm of the world; the larger patterns define your general direction, but you never know quite what to expect as each line changes.

Back out on the streets, driving home, we passed through the inevitable army checkpoints and were pulled over for a routine search. An Ulster Defence Regiment soldier frisked my legs and asked me how I liked "Norn Iron," Northern Ireland; it was an interesting place, I said. "Sure, it's a very friendly wee province, isn't it?" he said, as he moved his hands upwards towards my inner thighs. I could only agree that it was, indeed.

At first, you notice every gun. After a while, they become part of the scenery. I am not sure whether this is a good thing or not.

Belfast has its larger patterns, which define the direction of your life, but you never quite know what to expect as each line changes. The words of Charles Gavan Duffy come to mind: "A nation rarely changes its character, and in Ireland hitherto history has repeated itself with the fidelity of a stock piece at the theatre, where nothing is changed from generation to generation but the actors." He wrote that back in 1883. The patterns are carved in history; history is a prison, history is a trap. You could take the sectarian killings in South Armagh and trace them at least as far back as the conflict between the Catholic Defenders and the Protestant Orangemen in the late-eighteenth century; if you look closely enough, you'll even find that the same families were involved on each side. Or you could take the Belfast riots of 1969, and find the same flashpoints and the same fighting in the same streets as in the Belfast riots of 1869. James Maurice Craig put it in verse:

> O, the bricks they will bleed and the rain it will weep
> And the damp Lagan fog lull the city to sleep.
> It's to hell with the future, and live on the past;
> May the Lord in his mercy be kind to Belfast.

In some ways, though, there is no past at all in the North; there is only an eternal present, in which rival atrocities from the 1640s or the 1790s fuse with rival atrocities from the 1920s or the 1980s, in which events, memories and myths have become jumbled together in contemporary consciousness, in which the dead and the living are chained together.

This fusion of past and present derives much of its power from the sheer strength of community consciousness in the North. Each group has closed ranks against the other, and the extremism of one side has become the justification for the extremism of the other; the finger of blame is always pointed at the enemy, and responsibility for violence is routinely shifted onto the other side's shoulders. When an IRA bomb goes off in a crowded street, the deaths may be seen as "regrettable," but it is the "British presence" which is to blame; when the Loyalist paramilitary Ulster Freedom Fighters spray a Catholic betting shop with bullets, it is the "Republican war machine" that is to blame – so many killers, convincing themselves that they and their community are the real victims.

For the next few days, I stayed with a family in the Catholic Falls Road district, to get some sense of the view from the inside. They hadn't always lived on the Falls; back in the mid-1950s they bought a house in a "mixed," Protestant and Catholic, area of Belfast. Both their next-door neighbours were Protestants and they got on well together; their children would even make tea for the men returning home from the local Orange Lodge. But in 1972, one of the worst years of the Troubles, all that changed. Protestant paramilitaries from a nearby housing estate began firing bullets and petrol bombs into their house, to "force out the Micks." The family hung on for three months; it was their home, they'd lived there for eighteen years, and at first they simply refused to budge. In the end, though, fears for their children's safety made them get out. It meant giving up all they had worked for. They sold the house for a pittance and moved into rented accommodation among their "own" people in the Falls.

We talked in their living room; the TV was permanently on, the front door was always open, and the kettle was never off the stove. People kept drifting in and out from down the street, exchanging news, drinking thick brown tea, checking out the visitor. As they looked back on the events that brought them into the Falls, the family spoke calmly, almost in a matter-of-fact fashion. At the time, they felt a mixture of emotions – fear, bitterness, sadness, and above all frustration at being uprooted, at losing control of their lives. The children, some now in their early thirties, remembered moments of terror, crouching on the floor clutching the rosary and praying that they'd survive. Now, distance has brought a measure of detachment. "Worse things have happened to other people, on both sides," said one.

Different districts of the Falls have different political shadings. The street where they lived was generally regarded as "Provo territory." They'd been there for less than a month, and were half-way through renovating and decorating the place, when the British Army came. A new family in a Provo street was a natural object of suspicion; the soldiers systematically went through the house, searching for arms. In the process, floorboards were torn up, panels were pulled open, and the work of renovation was destroyed. No weapons were found. The family applied for compensation, and were offered all of two pounds. The mother's response was predictable: "I told them to keep the money and buy toilet rolls with it," she said.

Since then, they have seen a number of British regiments policing the district and have experienced more arms searches. "Some of the soldiers are all right," said the father, "but others try to needle and provoke you into doing something stupid. Most of them are just kids, don't have a clue what's going on here, and want to be somewhere else." His strongest anger is directed not at the British Army, but at the locally based Royal Ulster Constabulary and the part-time Ulster Defence Regiment, who do know what's going on and who have nowhere else to go. The Ulster Defence Regiment in particular he sees as simply an organization of Protestant bigots in uniform. He remembers the time that a patrol searched the house of a Provo down the street who'd blown himself up with his own bomb; as they were going through the place in front of his parents, the soldiers were singing the Dave Clark song "I'm in pieces, bits and pieces." One of the daughters in the family, a secretary who cares nothing about politics, left no doubt about her own feelings: "I'll never trust a policeman or a soldier again," she said.

Out on the street, I met some of the kids in the neighbourhood – kids with raw energy and nothing to do, kids who laughed easily and fought easily, kids who were full of enthusiasm and anger and exuberance. "Mister, d'ye want a plastic?" asked one, offering me a plastic bullet fired by the police after a riot in the area; he insisted that I keep it, as something to remember him by. He and his mates talked excitedly about brickin' the Brits and how to make petrol bombs. "Have you ever met any Protestants?" I asked. "Protestants?" one replied, scrunching up his face and trying to think. "Well, there was one once, and he was walkin' up the street, and he was a Protestant. He was carryin' a big bottle of cider, and he was walkin' up the street. And once he got round the corner, he meant to throw the bottle at people, and then he dropped it, and everybody started brickin' him. And he run down back the street." "Is that the only Protestant you've seen?" "Yeah."

Later in the day, in a housing estate up the road, a young girl took me through the debris. "They were shooting plastics and they were firing petrol bombs," she said, "and there were some bombs, and a bomb went off this morning as well." "So what do you think of the soldiers and the police and the army?" I asked. "They're pigs. We hate them." "What have they done to you to make you hate them?" Her eyes began to water. "They put my daddy in jail." "How long was your daddy in jail?" "Two years," she said, choking back the tears. A little boy who'd tagged along beside her called out to be included: "They put my daddy in jail, too."

"Whatever you do," said the folks I was staying with, "whatever you do, don't go to the Shankill Road." Applied to themselves, it was sound advice; as a Catholic, you would not want to run into the wrong people in the heart of Protestant West Belfast. But for a visitor, it's a different story – although strangers are treated with more suspicion in Loyalist than in Republican districts. Such feelings of distrust reflect a general sense in the Protestant ghettoes that everyone is against them, that the whole world agrees with the Catholic case. The Catholics, according to the Protestant stereotype, are smooth talkers, subtle propagandists who have managed to turn world opinion against the plain-speaking honest Ulster Protestant people.

In some ways, staying in the Shankill is strikingly similar to staying in the Falls. There is an equally strong sense of community – people coming in and out of each other's houses, checking out the newcomer, telling you what's going on, venting their frustrations. But there's a different kind of defensiveness here, a sense of exasperation and helplessness and isolation, coupled with a fear of betrayal. The IRA are trying to bomb them into a united Ireland, they say, and nobody cares – not even the British themselves. "The British don't want us any more," I was told over and over again; "they'd like to get rid of us if they could." "See the English papers," one woman said, her voice shaking with anger. "When a bomb goes off in London, or the terrorists kill an English soldier, it's all over the front page. But when the bombs go off here, and our boys are blown to bits or shot, there's nothing at all. Nothing. It's like it never happened; it's like it just doesn't matter." Any talk about peace initiatives scares them; there's a lot of talk about the thin end of the wedge. If you make concessions to the nationalists, they say, you are rewarding and encouraging IRA terror; concessions will only lead to more killings and more demands, until the ultimate goal of a united Ireland is reached. Better draw the line now and stand by the old watchwords: No Surrender, Not an Inch.

The people who should hold that line, in their view, are the Royal Ulster Constabulary and the Ulster Defence Regiment – the very groups that are hated in the Falls as Protestant bigots in uniform. But it doesn't take long before you come to realize that the security forces are hated in the Shankill as well – although for very different reasons. "Who was it," one man asked, "who stopped us from parading through Catholic areas, who started clubbing us when we marched against Dublin rule, who put their pay packets above their patriotic duty to Ulster? The RUC, that's who." During the protest campaign against the Anglo-Irish Agreement of 1985, when Loyalists had petrol-bombed policemen's homes, he remembered flinging his change at the feet of a police reservist, thirty pieces of silver for a Judas. "SS – RUC," the kids would chant, while their parents told horror stories about people who'd been hit by plastics. At times, you had to pinch yourself to remember that this was Loyalist, not Nationalist west Belfast. "You can talk about the

Provies," one man said after he'd got a few pints under his belt. "Well, I'll tell you this: I'd walk hand in hand with a Provie any day to kill a cop." He told me of his reaction to the murder of a policeman shot in front of his twelve-year-old son by the IRA earlier in the week: "I thought to myself – good, one less of them bastards to worry about."

While many Loyalists condemn the police for attacking their "own" people, they also criticize them for being "soft" on the IRA. "The IRA say they're at war," one man told me, "and meanwhile our lot are going around playing toy soldiers. A policeman is a 'legitimate target' for the IRA when he's at home sitting watching the TV with his wife and children. He's a 'legitimate target' when he's out at the pub, having a drink. He's a 'legitimate target' when he's out doing his shopping, and he's a 'legitimate target' when he's in the street with his gun, doing his duty. Now, if that's the case with the people the IRA are opposing, then I think you've got to move to a situation where the terrorists feel exactly in the same position, where they're being harassed, where they feel that day in and day out they're under the same threat. And if that means a shoot-to-kill policy of known terrorists, then I wouldn't have any problem with that." But the security forces weren't being allowed to do their job, he said, and that was why the Loyalist paramilitaries were stepping in, to do it for them.

There were "decent Catholics," it was true – ones who worshipped quietly at their altars, behaved pretty much like decent Protestants, and supported the union with Britain. But most Catholics, he was convinced, supported or sympathized with the IRA. And you could never be quite sure whether you were dealing with a decent Catholic or a disloyal troublemaker – someone who would feign friendship while passing on information to the terrorists. "Never trust a teague, a Catholic, that's my motto," he said; "it's just safer that way."

The levels of trust go down, and the notion of an "innocent civilian" becomes narrower as well. While the IRA define a "legitimate target" as anyone who aids or abets the "forces of occupation," Loyalist paramilitaries such as the Ulster Freedom Fighters define a "legitimate target" as anyone who aids or abets the IRA –

including anyone who might have voted for Sinn Fein, the political wing. It was always possible, of course, that the UFF might make mistakes and shoot the wrong people, but bloodshed was a cleansing and a sanctifying thing, and the nation which regards it as the final horror has lost its manhood.

And so it goes, two sides locked in this destructive dance, determined that their own national anthem will be sung at the end of the night. The more I think about it, the more it seems that these Troubles are a kind of dark, malign mirror image of everything I love about this place. The sense of community that is so attractive and appealing starts to reveal a sinister side. The communities define themselves against each other, and feed the fears and fantasies that keep the conflict going; they are mutually exclusive, and they are mutually deforming. It's the same with the sense that travelling is more important than arriving, that meaning lies in the process rather than the product. With the music and the story-telling and the sense of humour and the cycling, the journey becomes its own justification, the means become ends in themselves. But there's a way in which this is also true of the Troubles. You can analyse them in terms of ethnicity, religion, colonialism, or class, but in doing so you can miss an important aspect of the reality – that they, too, have become their own justification, and that their means have become ends in themselves. In the end, if there is an end, the Troubles are about the Troubles; the magic rings have become vicious circles.

But if there are laments there are also songs; if there are slow airs, there are also jigs and reels. In the midst of all the nonsense, all the foolishness, people still drink together and laugh together; there are specks of colour in a desolate rockscape. The Belfast story-teller and yarnspinner Sam McAughtry once told me about a friend of his, the last Loyalist in the Republican New Lodge Road, who would go into his local pub every night and always sit in the same seat. If anyone else was sitting in that seat, even if it was a Provo for all he knew, the man would just stand and stare at him bleakly until it was given up. Opposite the pub, there was an Army Observation Post, where the soldiers would peer through telescopes and watch the street. At night time, he'd go out with his arm around some of the Catholic customers there, they'd stand up and make faces at the British Army post, and they'd strike poses like Spanish dancers, just in case the soldiers were taking their photographs.

Or again, there was Sam's friend wee Ted, a Catholic who wound up in a Protestant bar during the afternoon of the Twelfth, when the Orangemen were coming back from their parade. He knew that the Orangemen at the end of the march always took off their sashes and folded them neatly in brown paper parcels, before leaving for home. After thinking about it for a bit, he decided that he would go next door to the bakery, get himself some brown paper, and let on to be an Orangeman himself, just for the crack. When the marchers came into the pub, he went up to the bar, brown bag under his arm, and ordered his drink. "By God," he said, "that was some walk. Eight miles there and eight miles back, and a wee man like me. And my feet are slaughtering me. Give us a pint of Guinness there." And before he knew it, one of the Worshipful Purple and Black Orange Grand Masters came up to him and said "You were the smartest man on parade." One after another, the Orangemen started praising him to the skies and were sending him up half-uns of whiskey until they knocked him full drunk, and he had to be carried out into a taxi. It was only when he got home and sobered up that he realized he'd been wearing the *fáinne* on the lapel of his jacket, a little gold ring indicating to all who could see that he was a Gaelic speaker and Catholic. And every Orangeman in the pub had cottoned on to this straight away, and the whole lot of them had entered into the spirit of the thing because the march was over and they appreciated a good joke when they saw it.

So it takes all sorts, as they say; there are circles within circles, rings within rings, while the wheels of the world keep rolling down the road.

Whitehead: Reprise

The wheels took me past the northern estates of Belfast, beside
Rathcoole and Bawnmore, along the edge of Belfast Lough to
Carrickfergus, and over country roads to the hill overlooking
Whitehead, my finishing point. Through the brambles and the
blackberry bushes, I can see the bay, the railway line leading to
Larne, and Blackhead Lighthouse in the distance. I freewheel down
towards the turn to Whitehead, effortless cycling after so much
effort, floating on soft waves like a lost wooden ship lapping home
to the shore. I sit in the village café and drink my coffee slowly. I
wheel my bicycle back to the sea and slide my hands along the
railings, and watch the fishing boats and the ships going out from
Belfast harbour.

I feel tired, I feel weary, I feel wonderful, and, in a way, I feel
home. The family I'm staying with fix me up an Ulster Fry; the
lads take me out to the Whitecliff for a welcome-back pint. Houdini asks me to play in Hooks's Bar again and wants to know if I
ever learned "American Pie" on my travels. After a while, I took
the bicycle and the whistle, and walked once more along the
strand by the caves and the cliffs and the rocks below Blackhead.
Elderly couples passed by, crinkled smiles on ruddy faces. In the
place where the path turns upwards to the lighthouse, I went
down with the bicycle to the rock-pools and the sea-stacks, and
sat there in silence. The waves pulled back against the stone; sea-
birds circled on a sea-breeze. There was a soft wind from the
south, the last sign of summer. I turned towards the Scottish sea,

so that the sun would warm my back and the whistle would be sheltered from the stream. One day, I would return to this place. I started to play "South Wind," a slow, peaceful, melancholy air, a lament and a song, while the notes drifted over the water and dissolved into the sea.

Acknowledgments

I have made so many friends and received so much help in the course of writing this book that a full acknowledgments section would threaten to become as long as the text itself. In Whitehead, I thank Paul and Cathy Cole for their hospitality and for introducing me to the Otherworld of the fleadh cheols, that land of Eternal Youth where the music and Guinness and crack go on forever. Thanks also go to the Haveron family, for the generosity of their spirit and the warmth of their welcome, to say nothing of their mad sense of humour.

In Belfast, I have many happy memories of musical evenings with Jacynth Hamill, Carol Parker, Sean MacKay, Jacinta Meenan, Heather Innes, Christina Moore, Sean Holland, Eileen MacLaughlin, and the denizens of the old Sunflower Folk Club, from Jeff Harding and Jim Lillie to Rory the Barman, Adrian Cameron and Betty Griffin were regular companions at the Tuesday night Rotterdam Sessions, where you could hear some of the best traditional music in the world. Jan Harbison, then at the Institute of Irish Studies, shared with me her knowledge of and enthusiasm for the music of Ireland's harpers. Sam McAughtry told me enough stories in the space of one afternoon to make me feel that I'd lived in the city all my life. And Liam Kennedy, historian and peace activist, not only provided me with a place to stay but also became one of my closest friends; the late-night kitchen discussions about life, love, and politics over too many whiskeys were a wonderful part of my time in Ireland.

In Dublin, Carla King did not realize what she was starting on the day she gave me a tin whistle and the Francis McPeake *Pocket Tin Whistle Book*; I thank her for the presents and for putting up with my practising.

On the road, special thanks go to Marion Crawford and her family at the Ammiroy Bed-and-Breakfast in Ballycastle; to Ivor Ferris from Derry, who is possibly the most dedicated fleadh-goer on the island of Ireland; to Maura Kilfeather from Sligo, whose love for traditional music and great spirit made my stay there so enjoyable; to Irene Whelan and her family in Clifden, for guiding me through the Arts Festival and introducing me to their friends in town; and to Suzanne Hannon of the Leagard Bed-and-Breakfast in Miltown Malbay, for making me feel so much at home.

In Canada, I received much encouragement from a variety of friends who share my interest in music, writing, and Ireland. Greg Forbes and Gini Milligan, who walked around Ireland in the 1970s and learnt the music as they travelled, inspired me to make my own journey to the country. Roger James, troubadour, jester, and performer (among many other things) of "Gilligan's Island," taught me his songs and made me laugh a lot. Marie Anderson and Debbie Twiddy of the now-defunct Nearly Famous Folk Group were great fun to work with, although Marie still turns pale whenever she hears "Danny Boy." At the Canadian Broadcasting Corporation, I thank Alison Moss, David Cayley, and Bernie Lucht for their support. Christopher Moore offered valuable suggestions about getting the book published, as did Paul Farrelly of the Ireland Fund of Canada; their help is deeply appreciated.

The historical excursions in the book were influenced by conversations with Don Akenson, whose arguments never fail to sting and stimulate, and with Mary Daly, Cormac Ó Gráda, and Jim Donnelly, whose sometimes conflicting interpretations of Irish social and economic history are informed by a common intellectual integrity and depth of knowledge.

One of the delights about writing this book has been the way in which my friends and colleagues in the Celtic Studies Programme at St Michael's College, University of Toronto, have been a constant source of support. They have taken a great deal of interest in the book at every stage of its development, and responded positively to the entire project. Such attitudes are rare in the cut-throat world of academia, and I count myself extremely fortunate to work with such people. In this respect, I take great pleasure in thanking Ann Dooley, the program director, Máirín Nic Dhiarmada, and Jean Talman; I also appreciate the support of Jo Godfrey, Honorary Celt, at the principal's office.

The students in the Celtic Studies Programme are among the best I have ever taught; the level of commitment, enthusiasm, and intelligence they bring to their work is truly remarkable, and I have learned a great deal from them – more than they probably realize. In particular, I thank the students of SMC 346, Celtic Folklore and Music, for their ideas, their insights, and their imagination.

A very special word of thanks goes to Zsuzsa, who gave me marvellous moral support throughout the writing of the book, who commented constructively on the passages I insisted upon reading to her, and who agreed to marry me after a particularly fine Celtic music concert one night in Toronto. Without her, I would have had a different tale to tell, or maybe no tale at all.

Finally, I thank the men and women who play the music, for the joy they have brought into so many people's lives, on those magic nights when the crack goes up to ninety.

None of the people mentioned above is remotely responsible for a single word of the book, whether there be a truth or a lie in it.

A Note
on Sources

If you want to find out more about traditional Irish music, by far
the best book is Ciarán Carson's *Irish Traditional Music* (Belfast
1986); it's lively, entertaining, informative, and opinionated, and
perfectly captures the spirit of the sessions. For a more "theoretical"
approach to the structure of the music, I'd recommend Tomás Ó
Canainn, *Traditional Music in Ireland* (London 1978). Breandán
Breathnach's *Folk Music and Dances of Ireland* (Cork 1971) has some
useful material, but is also rather dry; the life and energy of the
sessions evaporates in the analysis.

Moving from the general to the particular, Joan Rimmer's *The
Irish Harp* (Cork 1969) traces the origin and development of Ireland's national instrument, and Donal O'Sullivan's *Carolan: The
Life, Times and Music of an Irish Harper* (London 1958) provides an
excellent account of its greatest composer. Sullivan's book also
includes the memoir of Arthur O'Neill, an eighteenth-century itinerant harper, which takes us into a lost musical world that is at
once strange and familiar. On the place of the harp in the late-
eighteenth-century Celtic Revival see Gráinne Yeats, *The Harp of
Ireland* (Belfast 1992). It would also be well worth looking at
Norman Vance, "Celts, Carthaginians and Constitutions: Anglo-
Irish Literary Relations, 1780–1820," *Irish Historical Studies* 87
(March 1981):216–38.

My discussion of Michael Coleman, the Sligo fiddler, was influenced by Harry Bradshaw's booklet, *Michael Coleman, 1891–1945*;
it's published along with two remixed cassettes of Coleman's music

on the Viva Voce label, released in 1991. For the song tradition in Ireland, and for a wonderful read as well, I'd suggest Paddy Tunney's *The Stone Fiddle: My Way to Traditional Song* (Belfast 1979); apart from anything else, you'll get the full story of Carolan and Denis McCabe surprising the poteen drinkers on All Souls' Night. The literature on Irish folklore and mythology is vast, but there are some specific works that I found particularly useful. Donald Akenson's *Between Two Revolutions: Islandmagee, County Antrim, 1798–1920* (Port Credit, Ontario 1979) has a marvellous chapter on the island cosmology, and P.G. McBride's *Watertop: Where the Curlew Flies* (np 1992) is a good source of information for the lore and life of the Glens of Antrim. Máire MacNeill, *The Festival of Lughnasa* (London 1962), is also well worth consulting. On the storytelling tradition, two of the best books are Henry Glassie, *Irish Folktales* (New York 1985), and Sean O'Sullivan, *Folktales of Ireland* (Chicago 1966). For a good mixture of mythology and folklore see Robin Williamson, *The Wise and Foolish Tongue: Celtic Stories and Poems* (San Francisco 1991). I should also here declare my indebtedness to Jeffrey Gantz's translation of the Welsh mythological stories *The Mabinogian* (Harmondsworth 1976), John Millington Synge's *The Aran Islands* (1907; Harmondsworth 1992), and James Joyce's "The Dead," in *Dubliners* (1916; Harmondsworth 1976).

On the historical and political side, my views of the Easter Rising have been influenced by Conor Cruise O'Brien, "Revolution and the Shaping of Modern Ireland," in R. O'Driscoll, ed., *The Celtic Consciousness* (New York 1982). The discussion of the Famine drew principally on the work of Cecil Woodham-Smith, *The Great Hunger* (1962; Harmondsworth 1991), Mary Daly, *The Famine in Ireland* (Dundalk 1986), and Cormac Ó Gráda, *The Great Famine in Ireland* (London 1989). For the radical Irish fascination with revolutionary and Napoleonic France see Marianne Elliott, *Partners in Revolution: The United Irishmen and France* (Yale 1982). On the situation in Northern Ireland, Tom Wilson, *Ulster: Conflict and Consent* (London 1989), and J. Bowyer Bell, *Troubles* (New York 1993), provide useful overviews; for the situation on the ground, Sally Belfrage, *The Crack: A Belfast Year* (London 1987) is highly recommended. And for a good dash of Belfast humour see Sam McAughtry, *Blind Spot and Other Stories* (Belfast 1979).

And now, you have got the start and the finish of the story about Ireland, a bicycle, and a tin whistle. May you and your company be seven thousand times better off a year from today.

DATE DUE